DATE DUE

DE 22 '95			
DE 1 8 '0?			

DEMCO 38-296

Humanitarian Action
in Times of War

The Humanitarianism and War Project

*The Thomas J. Watson Jr. Institute for International Studies,
Brown University, and the Refugee Policy Group*

A HANDBOOK FOR PRACTITIONERS

Humanitarian Action in Times of War

Larry Minear
Thomas G. Weiss

Lynne Rienner Publishers · Boulder & London

Published in the United States of America in 1993 by
Lynne Rienner Publishers, Inc.
1800 30th Street, Boulder, Colorado 80301

and in the United Kingdom by
Lynne Rienner Publishers, Inc.
3 Henrietta Street, Covent Garden, London WC2E 8LU

Library of Congress Cataloging-in-Publication Data
Minear, Larry, 1936–
    Humanitarian action in times of war : a handbook for practitioners
    / by Larry Minear and Thomas G. Weiss.
        p. cm
    Includes bibliographical references and index.
    ISBN 1-55587-437-1 (alk. paper)
        1. War victims—Legal status, laws, etc. 2. International relief.
I. Weiss, Thomas George. II. Title.
JX5136.M56   1993
341.6'7—dc20   93-9825
                                                              CIP

British Cataloguing in Publication Data
A Cataloguing in Publication record for this book
is available from the British Library.

Printed and bound in the United States of America

The paper used in this publication meets the requirements
of the American National Standard for Permanence of
Paper for Printed Library Materials Z39.48-1984.   ∞

Contents

Preface

As codirectors of the Humanitarianism and War Project, we are pleased to make available this handbook as a resource to the international community.

Launched in 1991, our project has worked at the interface between theory and practice. We have found that as humanitarian concepts need to be informed by the day-to-day constraints confronting practitioners, humanitarian activities also can be strengthened by a more solid grounding in law, theory, and principle. This volume is part of that multifaceted effort to link conceptual analysis of humanitarian issues with practical recommendations to improve humanitarian programs.

While we have not shied away from producing scholarly articles on such topics as the erosion of national sovereignty and the evolving humanitarian regime, publications such as this one are also an integral part of our efforts. This handbook reflects our conviction that policy research that does not benefit practitioners—in this instance, humanitarian workers with dirty fingernails—will be poorer as a result.

First, we would like to record our debt to many organizations that have made possible the Humanitarianism and War Project. Above all are the two cosponsoring institutions: Brown University's Thomas J. Watson Jr. Institute for International Studies in Providence, Rhode Island, and the Refugee Policy Group of Washington, D.C., which have provided us with essential intellectual encouragement and administrative support. We acknowledge in particular the contribution of Dennis Gallagher, RPG's executive director.

Support from a wide array of sponsoring organizations has been indispensable to our undertaking, and in its diversity has helped assure comprehensiveness, independence, and balance to our work. Contributors currently include four governments (the Netherlands, France, the United Kingdom, and the United States); six UN organizations (UNICEF, UNHCR, SEPHA, DHA/UNDRO, UNDP, and WFP); ten nongovernmental organizations (Catholic Relief Services, Danish Refugee Council, the

International Center for Human Rights and Democratic Development [Canada], International Federation of Red Cross and Red Crescent Societies, Lutheran World Federation, Lutheran World Relief, Mennonite Central Committee, Norwegian Refugee Council, Oxfam-UK, and Save the Children Fund–UK); and three foundations (the Pew Charitable Trusts, the Rockefeller Foundation, and the Arias Foundation).

The sponsorship indicates the breadth of interest in our work throughout the humanitarian community and reflects an unusual openness among practitioners to consider ways of improving the effectiveness of their efforts. It also represents a strong vote of confidence in the utility of independent analysis.

While not helping to underwrite our project financially, other organizations, including the International Committee of the Red Cross, Médecins Sans Frontières, the International Council of Voluntary Agencies, and the International Association for Voluntary International Action (InterAction), have shared their experiences with us, provided fora for discussions, and contributed in other ways to our work. In short, many key elements of the international humanitarian community have been involved in one capacity or another in this research initiative.

With respect to this handbook in particular, we wish to acknowledge the specific contributions of a number of institutions. The published version is the third draft in a process designed to stimulate maximum discussion of the issues among practitioners. Doubtless, it will itself need revision in the future to reflect subsequent experience and developments.

The handbook's first draft, built on the findings and recommendations of a 1990 case study of Operation Lifeline Sudan (and described in Chapter One), was circulated in early 1992, and discussed by a group of experts at Brown University in April of that year. A significantly revised version, dated May 1, 1992, circulated during the balance of 1992. That version stimulated additional suggestions for revisions, which are reflected in the current text.

The handbook also has benefited from meetings with practitioners in late 1992 in San Jose, Costa Rica, which were organized by the Center for Reconciliation and Peace of the Arias Foundation, and in Nairobi, Kenya, by the Ecumenical Support Program. We would like to thank our friends and colleagues Luís Guillermo Solís in Central America and Elizabeth Otieno in East Africa, who helped to make these meetings possible.

We also wish to acknowledge comments and suggestions from a host of individuals, too numerous to mention, whose efforts and experiences in conflicts around the world have provided grist for our analytical mill. We wish to thank their organizations, including the All Africa Conference of Churches, Catholic Relief Services, the Government of the Netherlands, InterAction, the InterAfrica Group, the International Federation of Red

Cross and Red Crescent Societies, Oxfam-UK, the UN Department of Humanitarian Affairs, UNHCR, and USAID.

The publication of this report in English, and later this year in Spanish and French, has been made possible by a generous grant from the Pew Charitable Trusts of Philadelphia and by a special contribution from the International Centre for Human Rights and Democratic Development of Montreal. Grant funds have enabled a print run large enough to accommodate bulk orders from organizations that would like to use the manual for staff training, and to keep the price of single copies affordable. Additional information on purchase arrangements and reproduction rights of portions of this handbook is available from the publisher.

We view this handbook as a work in progress. It reflects the research carried out as of the end of 1992 by the Humanitarianism and War Project and comments made by organizations and individuals along the way. A number of examples are drawn from the Sudan and Gulf experiences. These are not necessarily more important than efforts to assist people elsewhere; they are simply better known to us by virtue of our research to date.

The issuing of this handbook at roughly the midpoint in the life of our research endeavor was made possible by the strong support from staff at both cosponsoring institutions. We would like in particular to acknowledge the contributions of Fred Fullerton, editorial associate at the Watson Institute, and Judy Ombura, research associate at the Refugee Policy Group.

As ongoing research will enrich and inform the contents of the handbook, we hope that other users will annotate the margins with their own experiences and adapt and revise the text to suit their purposes. We welcome comments about the handbook and suggestions for refinements and additional examples.

While acknowledging with gratitude the support from this wide array of institutions and individuals, we remain fully responsible for any shortcomings or errors in the text. For those interested in other publications of the project, there is a listing in the final section of the bibliography.

L. M.
T. G. W.

Abbreviations

CIREFCA	Conferencia Internacional Sobre los Refugiados en Centro-América
CRS	Catholic Relief Services
DAC	Development Assistance Committee (OECD)
DHA	Department of Humanitarian Affairs (UN)
EC	European Community
ECOWAS	Economic Community of West African States
FMLN	Frente Farabundo Martí para la Liberación Nacional
ICRC	International Committee of the Red Cross
ICVA	International Council of Voluntary Agencies
LWF	Lutheran World Federation
MSF	Médecins Sans Frontières
NGO	Nongovernmental Organization
OECD	Organization of Economic Cooperation and Development
OFDA	Office of Foreign Disaster Assistance (U.S.)
OLS	Operation Lifeline Sudan
RENAMO	Mozambique National Resistance
REST	Relief Society of Tigray
RPG	Refugee Policy Group
SEPHA	Special Emergency Programme for the Horn of Africa (UN)
SRRA	Sudan Relief and Rehabilitation Association
UK	United Kingdom
UN	United Nations
UNDP	UN Development Programme
UNDRO	United Nations Disaster Relief Office
UNHCR	United Nations High Commissioner for Refugees
UNICEF	United Nations International Children's Emergency Fund

U.S.	United States of America
USAID	U.S. Agency for International Development
USSR	Union of Soviet Socialist Republics
WFP	World Food Programme (UN)

Introduction

In recent years, widespread and endemic conflict has presented humanitarian agencies with formidable challenges. Whether between or within states, strife has increased both the need for humanitarian activities and the difficulty of providing them effectively.

The end of the Cold War has brought a gradual winding down of regional conflicts in which superpower involvement had added to the levels of human carnage. In such places as Nicaragua, El Salvador, Ethiopia, and Cambodia, attention is now turning from the need for emergency assistance to the medium- and longer-term tasks of economic development, social reconstruction, and political reconciliation. However, the menace of renewed hostilities remains an ever-present danger.

In Afghanistan, Mozambique, Angola, and Somalia, conflicts fanned by the Cold War have taken on a life of their own. In the former Yugoslavia, Albania, Tajikistan, and other republics of the former Soviet Union, tensions dampened by superpower rivalry are being rekindled. In the Sudan, Liberia, South Africa, East Timor, Sri Lanka, Lebanon, Colombia, Peru, and Israel and the Occupied Territories, conflicts with little relationship to the Cold War proceed apace. In short, internal tensions around the world are coming into their own as a growing source of instability and upheaval.

In many of these conflict areas, agencies seeking to provide assistance and protection have been buffeted by the prevailing insecurity. Like the persons in need of aid, agency personnel themselves have been harassed, held hostage, injured, and killed. Aid convoys have been hijacked or blocked, and aid activities commandeered or shut down. On occasion, insecurity and peril have prompted the deployment of military forces in support of assistance and protection activities, with varying results.

With past conflicts fresh in mind, with continuing conflicts presenting ongoing challenges, and with a conflict-laden future on the horizon, agencies that provide humanitarian assistance and protection are seeking to distill lessons from recent experiences. Agencies are aware that new levels

*T*he world into which we are moving will be infinitely more complex. Local conflicts will be more likely and, given modern technology, more lethal.
Henry Kissinger, former U.S. Secretary of State, 1991[1]

of professionalism are required to carry out their missions effectively. Consequently, they are reviewing fundamental humanitarian principles, rethinking philosophy and objectives, refining operational strategies, and seeking to equip staff better to function in armed conflict arenas.

The process of reflection is moving forward on a number of fronts. Developments in the United States are illustrative. Government agencies such as the U.S. Agency for International Development (USAID) are reviewing strategies for famine prevention and disaster mitigation in settings where civil strife complicates action. The U.S. Army is examining the experience of Operation Provide Comfort in the Persian Gulf. The Catholic Relief Services organization has developed a framework and practical guidelines to inform its response to conflict situations.

InterAction, the association of U.S. private voluntary organizations, had already begun the reflection process in the mid-1980s with a study, the findings of which are recapped in Larry Minear's book *Helping People in an Age of Conflict: Toward A New Professionalism in U.S. Voluntary Humanitarian Assistance.*

UN agencies are also analyzing recent activities. The UN Department of Humanitarian Affairs (DHA), created in early 1992, has been in the center of efforts within the United Nations to improve the coordination and effectiveness of humanitarian activities. UNHCR, through a newly established Working Group on Protection, has identified and discussed with its Executive Committee in 1992 changes in mandate and procedures to respond.

UNDP and DHA have embarked on a three-year disaster management training program that includes materials on assisting persons displaced by civil conflict. UNDRO provided special funding for a UN system-wide study by the Humanitarianism and War Project of coordination during the Gulf crisis, which is entitled *United Nations Coordination of the International Humanitarian Response to the Gulf Crisis, 1991–92.* In December 1992, DHA joined with the International Federation of Red Cross and Red Crescent Societies to sponsor a workshop at NATO headquarters in Brussels to discuss guidelines for governing relationships between national member societies and military forces.

In 1990, a number of governments, private agencies, and UN organizations joined together to support the case study of Operation Lifeline Sudan, noted in this volume's preface. The research resulted in a book entitled *Humanitarianism Under Siege: A Critical Review of Operation Lifeline Sudan,* which reviewed the dynamics of establishing and protecting the principle that, during an active civil war, civilian populations have a right to humanitarian assistance, and impartial aid agencies have a right to provide it.

The Sudan study also produced a *Report to the Aid Agencies,* which identified major institutional problems hampering more effective assistance in the Sudan and made a series of recommendations to address them. The findings were presented to NGOs in Nairobi and Geneva, to senior officials of UN agencies in New York, and to an expert consultation held at Brown University in April 1991. The results of the consultations were summarized in *Humanitarianism and War: Learning the Lessons from Recent Armed Conflicts.*

A consistent theme of the Sudan discussions was that the utility of the findings and recommendations of the Operation Lifeline study was limited by the special circumstances of that particular civil war and relief intervention. Caution was expressed about instituting improvements in the global system of aid and protection, based on experiences in a single conflict setting.

Reflecting encouragement received to review challenges presented by other conflicts, an expanded research initiative, the Humanitarianism and War Project, was launched in late 1991 by Brown University's Thomas J. Watson Jr. Institute for International Studies and the Refugee Policy Group. A broad cross section of UN, government, and private aid agencies underwrote the project, which is now seeking to distill the lessons to be learned from a wider range of country experiences.

The present study begins with the realization that, as the experts at the 1991 meeting observed, "when the international community mobilizes to assist famine threatened civilians in zones of armed conflict, it faces a set of generic problems, however idiosyncratic the particulars of a given situation." Generic problems also emerge from armed conflicts in which famine is not an issue.

This handbook follows up on the recommendation that a checklist for practitioners be drawn up, reflecting the experiences of agencies in a wider sampling of settings. A "checklist could indeed be a helpful tool," the group concluded, "for improving the effectiveness of aid activities and the accountability of the international system." It recommended that the conveners initiate a process, including practitioner workshops and additional case studies, through which such an instrument would be developed.

The document that follows is one of a number of activities being pursued by the Humanitarianism and War Project. Two other books are in process. The first is *Humanitarianism Across Borders: Sustaining Civilians in Times of War,* a collection of essays by nine authors, woven together by the project's codirectors' commentary on key conceptual, operational, and institutional issues in the development of a more effective international humanitarian regime. The second volume is *Humanitarianism and*

War: Reducing the Human Cost of Armed Conflicts. With the concerned international public in mind, it will present creative strategies of humanitarian assistance and protection from recent years.

This handbook was written with some assumptions that need to be stated at the outset. First, the humanitarian principles and policy guidelines presented are designed to be relevant for all the major civilian actors that directly provide humanitarian assistance and protection. Despite major differences in how UN organizations, donor governments, NGOs, the ICRC, and institutions in the conflict areas themselves approach their humanitarian tasks, we assume that all actors share certain basic commitments to certain humanitarian principles. These principles in turn provide a potential basis for agreement on ground rules for humanitarian action and a helpful benchmark against which to judge activities on behalf of civilians in armed conflicts.

Second, the handbook assumes that an effective humanitarian action in conflict settings will benefit from a clear and careful division of labor among actors. Necessary tasks include gathering data about the severity of the crisis; negotiating a framework for aid and protection; mobilizing the necessary resources; orchestrating humanitarian efforts; staffing and carrying out operations; and assuring appropriate accountability.

All agencies should not be involved necessarily in each task. Some agencies may have a comparative advantage in providing aid in the heat of battle or in fostering protection in a climate where suspicion prevails, while others may need to wait for the air to clear before taking the field. Some may enjoy a comparative advantage in a given region for reasons of history and language; others for technical competence or existing infrastructures. In pursuing comparative advantages, however, each agency has a substantial interest in the effective execution of all the necessary tasks by the humanitarian community as a whole.

Third, the handbook's focus is on situations involving interstate or internal wars or other armed conflicts. Many of the tasks enumerated are not unique to conflict settings, representing instead generic challenges to humanitarian professionals across a range of activities and operational landscapes. Some of the challenges are as integral to reconstruction and development work as they are to emergency lifesaving action. However, the difficulties in carrying out the stated tasks are heightened when strife is present.

For example, like their counterparts surrounded by war, aid workers providing shelter or potable water after an earthquake will have to precede their work by a needs assessment. The challenge of measuring the severity of the needs, however, is greatly accentuated when access to all areas in turmoil is not readily available. Similarly, coordination is never easy to structure or achieve because it involves complex issues both technical and political in nature. However, the normal difficulties of coordination are

War and armed conflict stand as the basic obstacle to eliminating famine in our time. It does not take a visionary to see that we are moving—crudely, roughly, hesitatingly, provisionally—toward a moment when we can separate out the starvation of humanity from the burdens of war. Humanitarian aid may be the leading edge of new and higher expectations of governments by the international public and of a greater sense of accountability for mitigating or, better yet, avoiding famine altogether.

Robert W. Kates, former director of Brown University's World Hunger Program, 1992[2]

heightened when an agency assuming a coordinating role is unable to maintain the necessary impartiality toward the belligerents, or even to keep open lines of communication with all of them.

Accordingly, the handbook focuses on the specific difficulties during conflicts of performing certain generic functions. Its utility will therefore be more limited for organizations preoccupied with so-called natural disasters or with longer-term development challenges.

Fourth, the handbook, for all its emphasis on common humanitarian principles, assumes that each agency needs to come to terms with these issues in its own right. However desirable the achievement of consensus across a community of highly diverse and idiosyncratic institutions, a lowest-common-denominator approach runs the risk of diluting key principles. People in life-threatening situations will be better served by a highest-common-denominator approach: that is, by one that seeks agreement among a narrower range of like-minded agencies.

Finally, as noted in the preface, the emphasis of the handbook—as well as of the Humanitarianism and War Project as a whole—is on creating a useful product to enhance operational effectiveness. The handbook takes care not to reinvent existing humanitarian wheels. It notes recent discussions that have taken place, comments on institutional changes already under way, and, in the bibliography, references available manuals and other resources. It seeks a middle ground between broad philosophical principles and pronouncements with limited practical application to operational challenges, on the one hand, and pragmatic strategies, with little relevance to overarching humanitarian principles, on the other.

This volume's working hypothesis is that those agencies that are clear and consistent in their articulation and observance of basic humanitarian principles will be more successful in their efforts than those that are not. Conversely, it suggests that those agencies operating on the basis of improvisation, unconstrained by fidelity to stated principles of action, will acquit themselves less well when tested on the anvil of conflict.

The principles discussed here are not moral absolutes but rather fundamental objectives toward which humanitarian action should be

The international community is moving toward codification of principles and identification of the appropriate conditions under which humanitarian imperatives will override domestic jurisdiction.
Jarat Chopra and Thomas G. Weiss, Watson Institute for International Studies, Brown University, 1992[3]

oriented. In humanitarian action, perhaps more than in other spheres of endeavor, there may be as many exceptions as rules. Yet principles establish benchmarks against which performance can be measured and help prevent energetic pragmatism from degenerating into unprincipled opportunism.

This handbook does not seek to provide "pat answers" for ready application to each situation. Nor, in seeking to distill collective lessons from diverse experiences around the world, does it treat those experiences as universal or prescriptive—they are presented instead as creative approaches that may be adapted to other circumstances.

The text is organized to reflect a necessary and healthy tension between principle and practice, between conceptual vision and operational realities. Certain themes recur as the text proceeds from framing principles to stating policy guidelines, and then to the level of their implementation. Chapter One identifies eight humanitarian principles, dubbed the "Providence Principles" after the location of the Watson Institute, with which actions should be consistent. Chapter Two provides a comprehensive set of practical considerations—in the form of a functional checklist, ingredients for agency decisionmaking, and operational strategies—to meet the challenge of more effective humanitarian activities. Chapter Three outlines a code of conduct for practitioners in settings of armed conflict for consideration by humanitarian organizations, both individually and as a community.

NOTES

1. Henry Kissinger, *The Washington Post*, February 26, 1991: A21.
2. Robert W. Kates, oral remarks to the Humanitarianism and War Consultation, the Watson Institute, Providence, R.I., April 8, 1992.
3. Jarat Chopra and Thomas G. Weiss, "Sovereignty Is No Longer Sacrosanct," *Ethics and International Affairs* 6 (1992): 117.

Chapter One

Guiding Humanitarian Principles: Toward a Framework for Action

Many agencies, public and private, currently provide humanitarian assistance and protection to civilians in situations of armed conflict. Some engage in activities spanning the relief-to-development spectrum or a range of sectors, such as food and nutrition, health and medicine, rescue and shelter. Others focus on one part of the spectrum or on a single sector. Some work exclusively at the community level; others are national and international in scope. Some have well-paid staffs and make use of the latest technology; others take a more no-frills approach to their work.

Despite differences in activities and styles, humanitarian agencies share certain broad objectives. At the heart of what they do is a basic commitment to improve the human condition. Some organizations tackle life-threatening human suffering directly, providing physical sustenance to refugees and displaced persons. Others take a more indirect approach, addressing the structural factors that create or exacerbate hunger, poverty, social conflict, and displacement.

This "war on children" is a 20th century invention. Only 5 percent of the casualties in the First World War were civilians. By the Second World War, the proportion had risen to 50 percent. And, as the century ends, the civilian share is normally about 80 percent—most of them women and children.
James P. Grant, UNICEF executive director, 1992[1]

Despite its core meaning revolving around a commitment to improve the human condition, the concept of humanitarianism in legal and colloquial usage over the years has been notably imprecise. In international law, the term "humanitarian" seldom has been delineated with the precision accorded such concepts as "human rights" or "refugee." The four Geneva Conventions of 1949 and the two Additional Protocols of 1977, the core of international humanitarian law, describe in great detail the humanitarian obligations of warring parties and of the international community. Yet what emerges is less definitional than descriptive and illustrative.

Similarly, one searches U.S. law in vain for a clear definition. U.S. foreign assistance legislation repeatedly speaks of humanitarian assistance but assumes, rather than specifies, what constitutes such aid. It was within this vacuum that the Reagan administration in 1985 requested, and the U.S. Congress approved, "humanitarian assistance" in the form of food, uniforms, and telecommunications equipment for the Nicaraguan insurgents.

The situation is hardly more clear at the international level. The UN Security Council's Sanctions Committee, in determining which items would benefit from the humanitarian exemption to the existing embargoes, has been hampered by a lack of clear international consensus on what constitutes "humanitarian." The resulting case-by-case review of whether such individual items as health kits, fertilizer, children's playthings, or spare parts for water purification plants qualify as humanitarian has been complicated by the injection of political agendas into the approval process.

Indicative of the absence of a generally agreed-upon definition of humanitarian assistance is the fact that one of the more frequently cited references is not from the Geneva Conventions or Protocols but from an interpretation of the International Court of Justice of the Conventions. Given a golden opportunity in the case brought by Nicaragua against the United States to fill the void with a crisp and eminently quotable definition, however, a divided Court declined. Finding against the United States in 1986, it referenced not international law per se but the principles of the International Committee of the Red Cross (ICRC).

If aid were to be authentically humanitarian, the Court reasoned, "not only must it be limited to the purposes hallowed in the practice of the Red Cross, namely 'to prevent and alleviate human suffering,' and 'to protect life and health and to ensure respect for the human being,' it must also, and above all, be given without discrimination to all in need in Nicaragua, not merely to the contras and their dependents." Rather than provide a quotable quote, the court itself made use of a quotation.

If international law fails to provide an all-purpose definition, everyday usage is even more diffuse. The *Oxford English Dictionary* of 1933 describes "humanitarian" as "having regard to the interests of humanity or mankind at large; relating to, or advocating, or practicing humanity or humane action." A second meaning, however, reflecting the more intrusive aspects of such concern, notes that the term is "often contemptuous or hostile."

"Humanitarian" still evokes multiple associations, from the strongly positive to the deeply negative. In some quarters, to call a person or an institution "humanitarian" suggests high praise and respect. Humanitarian organizations and individuals that stayed the perilous course in Somalia and eventually mobilized the world to act are deemed "heroic." Yet similar humanitarian action in the former Yugoslavia is criticized for having substituted for indispensable political and military action.

Similarly, Palestinians deported from Israel into southern Lebanon in late 1992 refused offers of humanitarian assistance, despite severe cold and hunger. "They did not want their cause to be turned into a humanitarian issue alone," one report observed. The association of humanitarian assistance with handouts and dependency gives such aid a pejorative ring in cultures in which "welfare," "charity," and "doing good" are loaded terms.

*T*he term "humanitarian" is employed in various ways in contemporary parlance. . . . At times it is used to denote a particular approach to problems, that is to say an approach that emphasizes protection and assistance to the individual as opposed to politically influenced considerations. At other times the term is used in a broad, generic sense and gives expression to a widely shared sentiment: anything that can be done to relieve human suffering and to help in the realization of human needs should be done.

Javier Pérez de Cuéllar, former UN Secretary-General, 1985[2]

In this handbook, the concepts of *humanitarianism* and *humanitarian action* are used delimitedly and expansively. The handbook notes that humanitarian action may have no extraneous agendas. At the same time, it views humanitarian assistance as encompassing activities covering a full spectrum, from the supplemental feeding of infants during famines to longer-term measures such as the strengthening of indigenous social and institutional coping mechanisms to avoid future crises. Similarly, humanitarian protection includes a spectrum of activities ranging from diplomatic efforts on behalf of an individual or group, to enhancing the safety of a vulnerable person or persons through international presence, to providing a physical barrier to deflect the threatened use of force.

At the core of all these humanitarian activities is relieving life-threatening human suffering and ensuring respect for human beings. Since human emergencies have roots in deep-seated economic injustice and in lack of respect for basic human rights, the underlying realities must be taken into account. Humanitarian action pursued in a contextual vacuum can have inhumane consequences.

This volume addresses the twin needs for greater clarity about the nature and objectives of humanitarian action and for greater attention to the necessary tensions between the relief of life-threatening suffering and the underlying causes of preventable human distress. The approach is positive and self-critical. If an activity is not humanitarian because humanitarians say it is not, neither is it ill-advised simply because it fails to prevent future human misery.

Although current definitions of humanitarianism are imperfect, the concept is developed most fully in the jurisprudence and cultures of Judeo-Christian nations. Many of the better-known humanitarian organizations are Western in origin and constituency. Their dominant ideology and style often have made humanitarian initiatives appear alien to non-Western countries in which major crises have occurred. Case studies carried out by the Humanitarianism and War Project of humanitarian activities in Jordan, Iraq, and Cambodia confirm that these efforts often have been mounted with too little attention to local values, traditions, and institutions.

At the same time, however, recent research and reflection also have demonstrated that the concept of humanitarianism is more universal, resonating with elements of religion, law, and ethics in other traditions across the globe. Humane instincts are not limited to persons who have reached a certain stage of economic or social development, nor are humanitarian institutions the unique creation of the Judeo-Christian West.

The preoccupation of Western legal and cultural traditions with individual political rights even may obscure the importance of economic and social rights in other cultures. The perceived obligations of extended families and communities to assist and protect the dispossessed may be a feature of non-Western traditions meriting greater attention in a more comprehensive approach to humanitarian values.

When a major human catastrophe strikes somewhere in today's global village, a bewildering bevy of organizations flocks into action. Often working side by side will be Christian, Muslim, and secular groups; persons from nearby communities and from halfway around the world; governmental, intergovernmental, and nongovernmental agencies; and civilian and military personnel.

While this all-hands-on-deck approach often works well, considerable confusion sometimes develops in certain instances, particularly where armed conflict is involved. When suffering is generated by war or exacerbated by conflict, humanitarian action takes place amid turbulence characterized by a high degree of politicization, insecurity, and military risk. Reaching people in such volatile surroundings can be not only difficult but also life-threatening.

The normal reaction to organizational confusion in the midst of conflict is to call for more effective coordination. Yet a closer look suggests that what may be needed is not, in the first instance, a clearer division of labor among actors. Disagreements that emerge under duress in the humanitarian theater frequently reflect instead underlying differences about what are fundamentally matters of principle.

Instead of the standard exhortations to coordinate and cooperate, greater clarity is first required concerning the principles underlying humanitarian action. The following analysis begins with a review of the overarching principles that guide action before moving to more operational matters. A clarification of goals and objectives—even if they command less than universal support and are difficult to implement in the rough and tumble world of realpolitik and military necessity—is the proper starting point.

This chapter of the handbook provides an overview of the international legal context for humanitarian action, some analytical categories, and finally an elaboration of humanitarian norms, labeled the Providence Principles.

INTERNATIONAL LEGAL CONTEXT

Discussions of humanitarian principle need to be situated within the context of international law. There is a well-established right for persons in need to have access to humanitarian assistance and, conversely, for impartial aid organizations to provide this assistance. Since its founding more than 125 years ago, the ICRC has played the key role in the codification, evolution, and dissemination of international humanitarian law.

"At least twenty provisions pertaining to armed conflict situations," states the ICRC, "deal with the food aid or medical assistance to which the victims of conflicts are entitled." The repository of the provisions, the four 1949 Geneva Conventions and the two Additional Protocols of 1977, oblige governments under stated conditions to allow the free passage of medical supplies, religious items, and other essentials to children under fifteen and to pregnant and lactating mothers (Fourth Convention, Article 23). The authorities are to eschew the use of "starvation of civilians as a method of combat" (Protocol II, Article 14).

Authorities are not allowed "to attack, destroy, remove or render useless objects indispensable to the survival of the civilian population, such as foodstuffs, agricultural areas for the projection of foodstuffs, crops, livestock, drinking water installations, and supplies and irrigation works for the specific purposes of denying them for their sustenance value to the civilian population or to the adverse Party, whatever the motive" (Protocol I, Article 54). The obligations detailed in the Protocols extend beyond governments exercising control over their own lands to powers occupying foreign or disputed territories.

Similarly, international law specifies that impartial aid agencies shall have access to populations in need. That access, however, is still subject to the consent of the authorities, even though in denying access those authorities act illegally. In a careful distinction between humanitarian initiative and political intervention, humanitarian law provides that "offers of such relief shall not be regarded as interference in the armed conflict or as unfriendly acts" (Protocol I, Article 70). Technically speaking, a humanitarian intervention is a contradiction in terms.

In a narrow sense, the Conventions and Protocols impose legal obligations only on those who have ratified them. As of December 31, 1992, 175 governments have ratified the Conventions, 119 Protocol I, and 109 Protocol II. In a broader sense, however, these texts have become the most widely accepted formulation—updated only fifteen years ago to reflect the evolving character of modern warfare—of the rights and obligations of states and other actors. Even some of the major powers that have not ratified the Protocols have incorporated key protections into their military manuals and training courses, suggesting the extent to which the stated principles have influenced the development of customary and conventional law.

The Geneva Conventions and Additional Protocols reflect a carefully calibrated balance between the human needs of civilians and the security needs of the ruling authorities. For example, the displacement of civilian populations is forbidden "unless the security of the civilians involved or imperative military reasons so demand." In these circumstances, however, "all possible measures shall be taken in order that the civilian population may be received under satisfactory conditions of shelter, hygiene, health, safety, and nutrition" (Protocol II, Article 17).

However clear the intention of the law, and however narrowly delineated the circumstances in which governments may be excused temporarily from their normal humanitarian obligations, respect is not assured. Nor does the Geneva Conventions' status as the most widely ratified international legal instrument guarantee their observance in the heat of battle or under the duress of domestic insecurity.

Moreover, the right to receive and to provide humanitarian assistance is less fully elaborated and less clearly monitored than are other comparable rights. In recent years, consideration has been given to establishing a humanitarian "regime" akin to those for human rights and refugee affairs, although in these areas monitoring and enforcement also remain less than satisfactory.

Current opinion is divided sharply on the need for new humanitarian law. Some experts believe that existing legal provisions are adequate, though more respect for already agreed-upon obligations is needed. Attempts to create new law would, they fear, end by eroding what is already on the books. In this context it is noted that certain provisions of the 1990 Convention on the Rights of the Child, the most recent attempt to strengthen safeguards, diminish the protections to which governments had already committed themselves in the Geneva Conventions and Additional Protocols.

Others hold that new provisions, or at least a more serviceable codification of existing provisions, are needed to increase the protections available to civilians in conflict settings and to those seeking to reach them. They point out that whatever the recently approved, specific provisions of the 1990 Convention, its creation served as an international consciousness-raising exercise, with multiple benefits for the status of children.

All agree, however, that the growing importance of humanitarian matters is a positive development, especially in the light of parallels to a growing concern with human rights. Prior to World War II, human rights were rarely considered a legitimate matter for international discussion. The Covenant of the League of Nations made no reference to human rights. During the interwar period, the subject was largely absent from the international agenda, except for an occasional debate in the International Labor Organization.

During, but more frequently after, World War II, many observers began to consider the embarrassing lack of international response to German and Japanese crimes against humanity. Since that time, one of the main arenas for discussion of these matters has been the United Nations. Most observers see the signing of the Universal Declaration of Human Rights in 1948 as a critical event in the redefinition of sovereignty in relation to humanitarian responsibilities. Since then, the burgeoning reality of interdependence in its economic, environmental, technological, and social dimensions has highlighted increasingly the porousness of national borders.

The United Nations Charter of 1945 itself contains a contradiction, or at least a tension, between sovereignty and human rights that is of pivotal importance for the evolving humanitarian regime. Article 2, upon which member governments place great emphasis, establishes as the cornerstone of the United Nations the principle of the sovereign equality of all member states. It prohibits the threat or use of force against any sovereign state and shelters from international scrutiny and action "matters which are essentially within the domestic jurisdiction of any state."

Yet other provisions of the UN Charter challenge the notion that state sovereignty deserves to remain absolute and uncontested. The preamble itself opens with the words: "We the Peoples of the United Nations determined . . . to reaffirm faith in fundamental human rights, in the dignity and worth of the human person, in the equal rights of men and women." Article 1 states that "the Purposes of the United Nations are . . . to achieve international cooperation in solving international problems of an economic, social, cultural, or humanitarian character, and in promoting and encouraging respect for human rights and for fundamental freedoms for all without distinction as to race, sex, language, or religion."

Articles 55 and 56 commit member states "to take joint and separate action in cooperation [with the UN to promote the] equal rights and self determination of peoples," a provision that includes "universal respect for, and observance of, human rights." In Article 68, the Economic and Social Council is called upon to "set up commissions . . . for the promotion of human rights." Article 76 affirms as a basic objective of the trusteeship system "to encourage respect for human rights and for fundamental freedoms for all." In this broader perspective, states have accepted international scrutiny of those major areas of national polity that they otherwise might seek to protect by appeals to state sovereignty.

Within the UN system, the rights of refugees have advanced steadily. The 1951 Convention relating to the Status of Refugees has provided a text as well as a large body of practice surrounding the work of the UNHCR. The obvious lacuna in the 1951 instrument regarding internally displaced persons, who in recent years have become far more numerous than officially recognized refugees, has created many conceptual and practical problems. But the recognition of the gaps in the 1951 Convention and in the 1967 Protocol is a step toward remedial action.

Tensions between noninterference in internal affairs of sovereign states and an active concern for human dignity wherever it is at risk have played themselves out during the history of the UN and in international relations since World War II. During those years, the balance between the two has evolved toward a more circumspect embrace of sovereignty and a more integral relationship between sovereignty and respect for human rights and humane values. As a result, once-sacrosanct state sovereignty is no longer an acceptable justification for violations of the rights of civilians in zones of armed conflict, if it ever was.

Half a century of tension between the principle of sovereignty and the growing concerns with humanitarian access has led the United Nations itself to examine the need for articulating and implementing the changing norms. The evolution is particularly evident in debates in recent years within the world's quintessential political forum, the General Assembly, where the political dynamics may be a more accurate barometer of world opinion than the views of World Court judges and academics. Indeed, UN resolutions may influence the actual application of international humanitarian law as spelled out in the Geneva Conventions and Protocols.

In 1988, the General Assembly adopted Resolution 43/131, which recognized the rights of civilians to international assistance and the role of NGOs in humanitarian emergencies. In 1990, Resolution 45/100 reaffirmed these rights and specifically endorsed the concept of corridors of tranquillity, cross-border operations, and other devices to facilitate humanitarian access. In April 1991, Security Council Resolution 688 framed the plight of some 1.5 million Kurds as sufficiently threatening to international peace and security to authorize outside military intervention and create havens for them.

In December 1991, General Assembly Resolution 46/182 requested the new UN Secretary-General to establish the position of an Under-Secretary-General for Humanitarian Affairs to coordinate humanitarian assistance. The resolution, which drew no distinction between victims of natural and of man-made disasters, required only the tacit "consent" of authorities rather than their explicit "request" to activate UN responses. Moreover, consent could come from a "country" experiencing such a disaster instead of from the "government" itself.

Today's international legal and political context for humanitarian activities is anything but static. Recent debates have been long and heated.

The passage of neither Security Council Resolution 688 nor General Assembly Resolution 46/182 was unanimous. Meanwhile, some governments, primarily those of developing countries, have been rethinking their support of the adopted formulations. Despite doubts, the assurance of humanitarian access has figured prominently in the authorization of force by the Security Council in Bosnia, Somalia, and Mozambique. Unanimous support for Security Council Resolution 794 in late 1992, introduced by African governments, paved the way for sending soldiers from twenty-one countries, led by the United States, to Somalia in Operation Restore Hope.

Some view the newly established UN mechanisms as administrative devices for assuring greater operational efficiency instead of more assertive mandates for humanitarian action. Others see movement toward recognition of a "right" of intervention to assure civilians of humanitarian assistance and to assure humanitarian agencies of access to them. Divergent interpretations notwithstanding, the direction of the evolving humanitarian regime is clear, even though specific elements, such as the criteria for triggering action and the mechanisms for enforcing compliance, require further discussion.

In short, the provisions of existing and germinating humanitarian law echo a social and moral sense widely shared across cultures that human beings should not be denied assistance and that food or other aid should not be provided, or denied, in the service of political objectives.

While respect for the fundamental sovereignty and integrity of the state remains central, it is undeniable that the centuries-old doctrine of absolute and exclusive sovereignty no longer stands, and was in fact never so absolute as it was conceived to be in theory. A major intellectual requirement of our time is to rethink the question of sovereignty.
Boutros Boutros-Ghali, UN Secretary-General, 1992[3]

ANALYTICAL CATEGORIES

The effort to equip practitioners to function during war benefits from the use of four analytical categories: institutional pillars; the nature of conflicts; phases within a conflict; and assistance and protection activities.

First, seven major actors form the *institutional pillars* of the international system of assistance and protection. On the international side, there are four: UN organizations, donor governments, NGOs, and the ICRC. On the domestic side—within countries experiencing conflicts—there are three: host governments, insurgents, and people's organizations.

Key roles also are played by other major actors, including the media and regional intergovernmental organizations, although generally not in the delivery of humanitarian services. Military forces, now increasingly providing humanitarian protection and assistance, are considered pillars by some analysts.

This handbook will be of interest to them, but they may have difficulty subscribing to some of the principles.

Even among the seven major recognized actors, there are significant differences in approaches to humanitarian assistance and protection. A host government and a UN agency have different responsibilities and constituencies. A UN official and an NGO staff person have different relationships with the host political authorities. The humanitarian wing of an armed insurgency has a different orientation than does the ICRC.

Within a particular category there are also differences. UNICEF has managed to deal more effectively with insurgents than most other members of the UN family. The Dutch Ministry of Development Cooperation and Nordic governmental aid entities have different perspectives and partnerships from those of USAID. The Mennonite Central Committee accepts no government funds, while government resources make up the largest single component of CARE's budget.

The handbook assumes that all actors share a basic commitment to humanitarian principles. The principles in turn provide a potential basis for agreement on common ground rules for humanitarian action and a helpful benchmark against which to judge activities on behalf of civilians in armed conflicts. References throughout to "the authorities" are used broadly to encompass political and military, government and insurgent elements.

A second category involves *the nature of the conflicts.* The warfare within which humanitarian institutions function covers a range of highly variable situations. Some are internal; others are interstate in character. Some are highly localized, with others countrywide or even regional in scope. Some have sputtered off-again, on-again; others have persisted for generations. Some erupt overnight, catching observers by surprise; others are long festering, the objects of scholarly analyses and early warnings.

Military technologies and strategies also vary widely. While some wars are fought with primitive means, most combatants today have access to sophisticated weapons. Some fighters are uniformed and highly professional, while others are ragtag irregulars and may include young children. Some armed forces restrict their targets and much of their devastation to military infrastructure. Others, particularly in so-called modern warfare, set their sights on civilian populations, local communities, and economic assets. Either way, civilians are affected.

Third, it is useful to identify *phases within any given conflict.* The war between the Ethiopian government and the Eritrean and Tigrayan insurgencies, for example, which continued over a period of more than two decades, included alternating periods of intense fighting and lulls, pitched battles, hit-and-run attacks, strafing, and mining before culminating in the capture of Asmara and Addis Ababa.

A progression in the violation of human rights may also be involved, particularly where the root cause of conflict involves the failure to work out mutually acceptable terms of coexistence among diverse ethnic groups. In the former Yugoslavia, for example, as the prevailing national cohesion frayed, there was an escalation in nature of the abuses, the blatantness of the violations, and the number of persons affected.

While every war complicates the work of humanitarian organizations, the specific nature and stage of a given conflict provides the landscape on which efforts to aid and protect civilian populations are mounted. Analysis of the dynamics of the military action and of the strategies and tactics of the belligerents may help humanitarian practitioners design more effective programs and prevent inadvertently worsening the plight of civilian populations.

Fourth, there is a *spectrum of humanitarian assistance and protection activities* that may be appropriate. The needs of civilian populations in El Salvador during the FMLN offensive in late 1989 were considerably different from those in early 1993 under the UN-brokered peace accords. Likewise, the needs of Salvadorans who began to move back from Honduras in 1987 were different from those of their Guatemalan counterparts, who in 1992–1993 were just beginning the repatriation process from Mexico. Such varying political and military landscapes provide highly variable backdrops for humanitarian responses.

Similarly, there is a spectrum of international assistance needed, ranging from short-term emergency relief through reconstruction of essential infrastructure to medium- and longer-term development. In recent years, attention has been directed increasingly to the interrelationships along the spectrum.

The general agreement is that emergency relief can affect the longer-term prospects of a recipient country, for better or worse. There is also consensus that relief should be provided in ways that seek to reduce a nation's vulnerability to future emergencies and its need for ongoing assistance. However, this is more easily agreed upon in theory than implemented programmatically. In actual practice, different agencies accord varying degrees of importance, ensuring that relief operations have a development orientation, support for local institutions, and nurturing collegiality with local partners.

Conflicts present difficult operational challenges and evoke different institutional responses. Some agencies see their major contribution in assisting the victims. Others concentrate on conflict prevention, endeavoring to head off outbreaks of violence. Still others, having developed greater expertise in conflict resolution, work in support of cease-fires and eventual peace agreements.

Among organizations concentrating on the delivery of emergency services, some are proven purveyors of assistance and protection while battles rage. Among these, the ICRC is perhaps the preeminent example. Others tend, sometimes for reasons not of their own choosing, to leave the scene

A rmed conflict, with the resulting violations of human rights, is by far the most pervasive cause of internal displacement and the resulting violations of human rights. . . . Often, mass dislocation occurs as groups seek to escape from physical danger and search for security and reliable sources of survival. However, displacement is the result of strategically or tactically calculated policies by the parties to armed conflict.
Francis M. Deng, special representative to the Secretary-General on Internally Displaced Persons, 1993[4]

until their personnel can come and go with reasonable safety. The UN in Somalia is an unfortunate but not atypical example. Still others elect to work in societies where structural violence and repression make access to civilians as precarious as during full-scale wars. The "watch" groups in the human rights area are such agencies. The need to identify comparative advantages and to be clear about an appropriate and serviceable division of labor is explored in the following chapter.

There are also complex conceptual, operational, and institutional linkages between providing emergency assistance and systematically assuring the protection of vulnerable individuals and populations. Recent experiences in northern Iraq and the former Yugoslavia have highlighted serious tensions between rendering assistance and providing protection. These are analyzed in the work of UNHCR's Working Group on International Protection and elaborated upon in the statement of the UN High Commissioner for Refugees, reprinted in Chapter Two.

These four basic analytical categories provide a highly complex and richly textured tapestry of human needs and humanitarian action. This fabric emerges from major international operations in such widely differing conflict settings as the Horn of Africa, Central America, the Persian Gulf, and Cambodia, which now are being documented in the research and publications of the Humanitarianism and War Project.

These categories also provide the context for the humanitarian principles detailed in the following section and for the policy guidelines for practitioners in the following chapter. The principles and guidelines that follow seek to distill some lessons from recent experience. Examples have been selected for their illustrative merit, not with invidious intent toward an agency or group of agencies. Agencies have a great deal to learn from one another, and the international community can benefit from efforts to provide more effective assistance and protection.

"PROVIDENCE PRINCIPLES":
EIGHT HUMANITARIAN GUIDEPOSTS

As noted in the introduction, the institutional pillars of the international humanitarian community, however divergent their structures and diverse

The Providence Principles of humanitarian action in armed conflicts are:

1. *Relieving Life-Threatening Suffering:* Humanitarian action should be directed toward the relief of immediate, life-threatening suffering.

2. *Proportionality to Need:* Humanitarian action should correspond to the degree of suffering, wherever it occurs. It should affirm the view that life is as precious in one part of the globe as another.

3. *Nonpartisanship:* Humanitarian action responds to human suffering because people are in need, not to advance political, sectarian, or other extraneous agendas. It should not take sides in conflicts.

4. *Independence:* In order to fulfill their mission, humanitarian organizations should be free of interference from home or host political authorities. Humanitarian space is essential for effective action.

5. *Accountability:* Humanitarian organizations should report fully on their activities to sponsors and beneficiaries. Humanitarianism should be transparent.

6. *Appropriateness:* Humanitarian action should be tailored to local circumstances and aim to enhance, not supplant, locally available resources.

7. *Contextualization:* Effective humanitarian action should encompass a comprehensive view of overall needs and of the impact of interventions. Encouraging respect for human rights and addressing the underlying causes of conflicts are essential elements.

8. *Subsidiarity of Sovereignty:* Where humanitarianism and sovereignty clash, sovereignty should defer to the relief of life-threatening suffering.

their constituencies, share a common commitment to the relief of suffering and the protection of human life. The following overarching principles represent a broad framework for international humanitarian action to which virtually all such institutions and practitioners can subscribe.

These principles are presented not as moral absolutes but as norms toward which to strive. Differences do and will exist: in the interpretation of particular principles, in the importance of some principles relative to others, and in the extent to which a given principle or principles will prevail in a given situation. Although extenuating circumstances may necessitate modifying a given principle, those who deviate from the norm should be aware of the costs. To repeat the working hypothesis: those who are clear and consistent in their articulation of principles will be more successful in their efforts than those who are not.

These principles represent fixed points on a shared compass. While not dictating unambiguous directions, they serve to stimulate discussion and provide a vehicle for greater cohesiveness and mutuality among practitioners. Vetted among humanitarian organizations and refined by users of this handbook to reflect new experience, they may serve as an agreed-upon referent against which future humanitarian action may be judged.

Relieving Life-Threatening Suffering

Humanitarian action should be directed toward the relief of immediate, life-threatening suffering.

The recent upsurge in life-threatening suffering, as noted in the introduction, presents the world's humanitarian system with formidable challenges. Dominating world news at the end of 1992 were reports from Bosnia of widespread misery and malnutrition, as well as death by freezing and rapes in the service of "ethnic cleansing." Vying with Bosnia for front-page coverage, with the displacement in former Yugoslavia of more than 2 million citizens, were deaths from starvation and civil strife of an estimated 300,000 to 500,000 people in Somalia.

But these were only the most attention-getting examples of extreme misery. Table 1.1 gives a panorama of some of the world's major war-related humanitarian crises at the end of 1992. It is the relief of life-threatening suffering from crises such as these that is the purpose of humanitarian action.

Elementary as appears the principle that humanitarian action should be directed toward the relief of immediate, life-threatening suffering, other agendas often have dominated. During the Cold War when anti-communist fervor infiltrated long-standing humanitarian traditions, the United States provided tents, boots, and communications equipment to the Nicaraguan insurgents under the rubric of "humanitarian" aid. The United States also committed "humanitarian" aid to other insurgencies seeking to topple communist regimes in Afghanistan, Angola, and Cambodia. Other major powers

Table 1.1   Humanitarian Crises Amidst War

	Population (million)		UN Emergency Appeals	
	Affected	Total	$ million	Period
Afghanistan	3.7	16.6	180	6–12/92
Angola	1.4	10.0	81	5–12/92
Ethiopia/Eritrea	9.2	49.2	200	7–12/92
Iraq	0.75	18.9	217	7/92–3/93
Liberia	2.1[a]	2.6	150	12/90–9/92
Mozambique	4.7[a]	15.7	250	5–12/92
Somalia	2.4	6.0	83	10–12/92
Sudan	7.8	25.2	141	7–12/92
Yugoslavia[b]	3.1	23.8	434	9/92–4/93

Source: United Nations Department of Public Information DPI/1320: "Enlarging the UN's Humanitarian Mandate," *United Nations Spotlight on Humanitarian Issues* (December 1992).
Notes: a. Including refugees in neighboring countries
b. Former

with less-established traditions of humanitarian assistance also aided selected regimes around the world to further their own political agendas.

The politicization of humanitarian action was contested by some within the U.S. government, by some NGOs, and by many within the international humanitarian community. They warned against compromising the integrity of bona fide humanitarian activities and jeopardizing the security of humanitarian personnel. Yet they failed to protect the cardinal principle of humanitarian action. Instead, the view expressed in a 1985 editorial in *The Washington Times* prevailed: "Anyone who examines the historical record of communism must conclude that any aid directed at overthrowing communism is humanitarian aid."

The waning of East-West tensions offers an opportunity to reaffirm the principle that the relief of immediate life-threatening suffering is valuable in its own right and to mobilize humanitarian action accordingly.

Proportionality to Need

Humanitarian action should correspond to the degree of suffering, wherever it occurs. It should affirm the view that life is as precious in one part of the globe as another.

One implication of the first principle is that humanitarian action requires engagement wherever major life-threatening suffering exists. All such suffering exercises a valid claim on internal or external resources. Arbitrary distinctions between instances of life-threatening suffering that

*H*umanitarian *assistance . . . is assistance provided in response to urgent and unmet basic human needs. It encompasses such items as food, medicines and medical supplies, shelter, clothing, water and basic household supplies delivered in a way that sustains people in need and enhances their potential to become self-reliant.*
InterAction Statement on Humanitarian Assistance, 1987[5]

exercise greater or lesser claims on international action undermine the universality central to a basic commitment to humanity.

While the notion of proportionality seems unobjectionable, the widespread nature of life-threatening suffering poses major difficulties of implementation. The stark reality is that more human suffering exists worldwide than any single agency—or for that matter, all agencies acting in concert—can alleviate. Although the Cold War meant enormous suffering for civilians in various regional and national conflicts, the waning of East-West tensions actually has been accompanied by an upsurge in violence.

The implications for an already overstretched humanitarian system are staggering. The U.S. government estimates that the geographical area within which USAID's Office of Foreign Disaster Assistance can be expected to respond to relief requirements has grown by 21 percent since the end of the Cold War. This translates into an additional 1.2 billion vulnerable people who may require emergency assistance.

That the issue of achieving at least a rough proportionality among allocations of international humanitarian assistance is a sensitive one is attested to by the reaction that greeted UN Secretary-General Boutros Boutros-Ghali's criticism of the Security Council in mid-1992 for being more preoccupied with human extremity in former Yugoslavia than in Somalia. In late 1990, the Security Council's preoccupation with Iraq's invasion of Kuwait preempted attention from the Liberian crisis, a far more serious humanitarian emergency at that time. The implication that a Somali life is less worthy of attention than a Kenyan life, a Burmese than an Afghan, a Haitian than a Bosnian, is an affront to fundamental humanitarian principles. Equity is essential.

Few organizations involved in humanitarian assistance and protection would hold that each of them individually should seek to be active in every country setting in which international involvement is needed. Most, however, would agree that the work of humanitarian agencies, taken together, should be in a general way proportionate to global need. Given difficulties in interagency coordination and collegiality explored later, achieving a well-balanced response to life-threatening suffering worldwide is a Sisyphean task.

Two other factors make more difficult the proportionate allocation of resources, whether by an individual organization or by groups acting together. The first concerns the perception of comparative need among parliaments and the concerned international public. Historical, cultural, ethnic, or political ties may create an imbalance in the interest expressed in various humanitarian crises. Disproportionate media coverage may also undermine efforts to assure evenhanded attention.

The second deterrent is the relative accessibility of respective crises. The human needs of Bhutanese refugees in Nepal are less visible than those of Palestinians in the Occupied Territories. Human rights violations in East Timor lend themselves less readily to monitoring than those in Nicaragua. Even accessibility within a given emergency may create a certain disproportionality. Thus Afghan and Cambodian refugees located inside the Pakistan and Thai borders and Liberians who sought refuge in neighboring countries received considerably greater attention than did their counterparts who were displaced within their countries of origin. In the first two instances, East-West political factors compounded the disparities in resource commitments.

In addition to questioning the integrity of humanitarian activities, disproportionate resource allocations dramatize the absence of an "invisible hand" to assure the necessary proportionality among humanitarian action across armed conflicts. In the late 1980s, about ten times more aid was provided from within Ethiopia to Ethiopians in the north than reached them across the Sudanese border. This reflected not only greater ease of access from within Ethiopia but also the preference of many UN organizations and donor governments for dealing with established governments rather than with insurgents. Although the aid provided to government-held areas was useful, the prevailing imbalance called its integrity into question.

Nonpartisanship

Humanitarian action responds to human suffering because people are in need, not to advance political, sectarian, or other extraneous agendas. It should not take sides in conflicts.

Devoid of specific political, religious, cultural, or other considerations, humanitarian action does not seek to promote a particular political or religious agenda, solidify the loyalty of a particular ethnic group or geographical area, dampen disaffection, or preempt insurrection. In keeping with the first principle, humanitarian action is mounted because civilians have a right and a need for such assistance.

While the prohibition against choosing sides in conflicts is unimpeachable in theory, this stricture can be especially difficult during international and internal wars. Not only do the warring parties frequently seek to prevent assistance from reaching the other side, but also they often treat outside aid and those providing it as endorsements of their cause.

Nonpartisanship is central to the ability of agencies to assist and protect persons on all sides of a conflict. Having endorsed the cause of the

*H*umanitarian *activities . . . must by defini-tion be disassociated from all shades of political considerations. They are, by definition, neutral and impartial. Only by preserving this pristine humanitarian character can we avoid that disagreements on political questions, or on all other questions, become impediments to emergency relief activities. Not by chance was the notion of humanitarian activities developed in connection with situations of armed conflict. The secret of effectiveness in the humanitarian field is that even when nations disagree on everything else, even when they clash, they can still agree that the wounded must be assisted, that the sick must receive adequate care, that suffering must be relieved. That is, if I may say so, a minimal straight line drawn in the crooked timber of humanity. It is the fact that agreement on such a core of minimum values is discernible, this fact and nothing else, that makes humanitarian action possible as such.*

Ronaldo Mota Sardenberg, ambassador of Brazil to the UN, 1991[6]

Tamil Tigers or the government of Mozambique, a humanitarian organization will find itself cut off from civilians in the territory of the Sri Lankan government or of RENAMO. Endorsement of one party in a civil war or in an electoral campaign makes the endorsing organization a target for the wrath of the opposition.

From March through December 1988, the ICRC carried out painstaking negotiations with the Khartoum government and the Sudan People's Liberation Movement before winning agreement for relief deliveries to an equal number of locations on each side. During a year when an estimated 250,000 persons died of war and famine, both sides were willing to deny assistance to "their own" civilians in order to prevent aid from reaching people in territory controlled by their opponents. The ICRC considers the principle of impartiality so important that it is unwilling to proceed without the agreement of all parties. This agreement also facilitates accountability and transparency.

Not all humanitarian institutions set such store on assisting on all sides of a conflict. Some fear that insistence on access to people everywhere may encourage the warring parties to prevent relief from being provided to people anywhere, or to seek to extract disproportionate amounts of aid. The Khartoum authorities insisted on a larger share of aid from Operation Lifeline Sudan for the areas that they controlled rather than according to strict proportionality. Taking such considerations into account, newly approved guidelines by Catholic Relief Services specify that "CRS prefers to assist victims on both sides of the conflict unless needs on one side are met by other groups or unless operational considerations preclude working on both sides."

Nonpartisanship, however, is not simply a strategy for achieving greater access to those in need. It is a matter of principle. Once humanitarian action serves causes rather than victims, once it embraces political parties or religious or cultural ideologies, it can no longer claim to be humanitarian or avail itself of international legal protections. It then loses its authentically humanitarian character, becoming precisely what the Geneva Conventions and Additional Protocols seek to avoid: an unfriendly act of interference in the conflict itself.

Insisting that humanitarian aid be free of extraneous agendas may appear naïve, given the mixed motivations that often figure in policy decisions. The importance of the principle at issue, however, is underscored by the regularity of its abuse. Humanitarian rationalizations often are invoked to justify interventions by such security-minded states as India in Sri Lanka, the Soviet Union in Afghanistan, Vietnam in Cambodia, and the United States in Grenada and Panama. The frequent use of humanitarian rationales as political rationalizations emphasizes the need for precision in the use of the term "humanitarian," not the least by humanitarian interests themselves.

These recent examples echo earlier rationalizations more reflective of power politics than humanitarianism. One of Japan's justifications for invading Manchuria in 1931 was humanitarian. Hitler's invasion of Czechoslovakia in 1938 claimed to protect ethnic Germans from mistreatment. Such abuses of human values help explain the reluctance of many developing countries, and the wariness among developed countries as well, to embrace the concept of humanitarian intervention.

Insistence on the nonpartisanship of humanitarian activities is not to deny their political ramifications or repercussions. Such activities may affect delicate political and military balances. They may have the effect of relieving authorities of responsibility to provide aid themselves; afford them greater freedom in using already existing resources for other purposes; and help them win enhanced respect from their own citizens and the international community for cooperating with aid efforts. While such political impacts are unavoidable, humanitarian organizations have an obligation to anticipate and monitor them.

Since any involvement in the highly politicized environment of conflicts, even for transparently humanitarian motivations, is likely to have political implications, it is important that humanitarian objectives be controlling. Yet experience attests to the reality that when multiple objectives exist, humanitarian considerations are frequently crowded out.

For that reason, organizations whose sole purpose is humanitarian have an advantage over institutions with multiple agendas and objectives. In this context, an organization such as the ICRC, whose only purpose is humanitarian, enjoys a comparative advantage over UN-related aid efforts. Humanitarian assistance provided by UNICEF and other UN entities in the wake of Iraq's invasion of Kuwait was compromised in the eyes of some recipients in Jordan and Iraq by its association with the economic sanctions and military actions authorized by the Security Council. For its part, the ICRC notified the Council's sanctions committee of shipments but did not request its permission. If some private institutions exist exclusively to provide aid and protection, they have a better chance than UN organizations or governments of keeping their actions free from extraneous agendas; however, the multiple responsibilities of intergovernmental and governmental agencies do not render their assistance by definition less than fully humanitarian.

Military forces have been playing a more active role in the humanitarian sphere in the early post–Cold War period. They have been involved in providing security for humanitarian operations and in delivering food, medical aid, and shelter. However unfair it may be to assert that military forces, whose reason for being is to prevent or wage war, are by nature unable to provide humanitarian aid, it seems self-evident that these institutions will have to work harder to keep human needs activities divorced from extraneous elements.

The principle of nonpartisanship elaborated on here is used in preference to the related principles of impartiality and neutrality espoused by the ICRC. It may seem unwise to bypass two principles referenced in international law and traditionally associated with humanitarian action in favor of the concept of nonpartisanship, which is without international legal standing. Yet there are significant reasons for this.

Most humanitarian organizations, while acknowledging the need not to take sides in conflicts, are at the same time reluctant to view themselves as impartial when fundamental issues of suffering are at stake. Confronted by apartheid in South Africa, indiscriminate use of force in Afghanistan, forced relocation of Guatemala's Indian population, or institutionalized poverty and violence in El Salvador, humanitarian organizations find "impartiality" not only impossible but also undesirable.

The CRS guidelines mentioned earlier make a commitment to impartiality "with respect to race, creed, political orientation, and ethnicity" and yet at the same time affirm the agency's partiality "to the poor, the suffering, and the marginalized." Moreover, advocacy activities of humanitarian agencies geared toward addressing the policies of governments that create or exacerbate such suffering are more consistent with nonpartisanship than with impartiality. These issues are explored in greater detail in the section of Chapter Two that addresses institutional benchmarks for action.

Independence

In order to fulfill their mission, humanitarian organizations should be free of interference from home or host political authorities. Humanitarian space is essential for effective action.

On the home front in donor countries, the need for independence means that international agencies receiving resources, whether from member

In conflict situations, respect for international humanitarian law is a prerequisite for an adequate response to emergencies. In terms of the existing right of the victims of armed conflict to assistance—a right which is often not known, ignored or misinterpreted—humanitarian assistance cannot be regarded as interference. While states have an obligation to facilitate assistance when the urgency of the needs makes it necessary, the task of the humanitarian organizations is to guarantee the impartial nature of such aid.
Cornelio Sommaruga, president of the International Committee of the Red Cross, 1993[7]

governments in the case of multilateral and bilateral programs or from public and private donors in the case of NGO programs, should not be constrained in carrying out their mandates. By the same token, in countries that host humanitarian activities, agencies must be free to carry out those activities without interference. Where home and host countries are the same—that is, for indigenous public and private humanitarian institutions—independence is equally essential but sometimes more difficult to assure. In short, adequate humanitarian space is needed for organizations of all types to function effectively and with integrity.

No humanitarian organization operating in conflicts has the degree of independence it wishes. It generally must operate with the approval, or at least the acquiescence, of local authorities. In one sense, this is no different from situations in which longer-term development assistance is provided. In another sense, however, the special nature of armed conflicts, in which relationships with political authorities are more highly charged and the presence of outside elements more sensitive, renders the need for independence both more acute and more problematic.

As with other principles, the minimum acceptable degree of independence will be judged differently by different institutions. An agency like the ICRC, which has no institutional links to any political entity, has intrinsically more freedom than an agency created by an insurgency to provide humanitarian services to civilians (for example, the Relief Society of Tigray [REST], an arm of the Tigrayan People's Liberation Front).

But there are also differences in the degree of independence enjoyed among insurgency-related aid institutions. REST had considerably more operational space than did its counterpart in the southern Sudan, the Sudan Relief and Rehabilitation Association (SRRA), a creation of the Sudan People's Liberation Movement. As a result, the institutions were able to function in a more or less humanitarian fashion, and international organizations were more or less prepared to work with one entity than with the other. Chapter Two explores some of the elements in determining whether the necessary degree of independence is present in a specific situation.

NGOs differ in the extent to which they believe they may accept resources from governments or UN agencies without compromising what they consider to be their necessary independence of action. These considerations led Oxfam-UK to set 20 percent as the upper limit for the value of contributions it accepts from governments in relation to resources donated from private sources. Other agencies have no such fixed percentage limit but instead make determinations on a case-by-case, country-by-country basis. Catholic Relief Services is not averse to having more than half of its budget made up of contributions from governments, provided that staff and indigenous partners have helped determine how such funds will be used.

Despite differences such as these in viewpoint and approach, there is general agreement on the principle that the ability of organizations to mount and sustain humanitarian initiatives without fetters is central to the concept of humanitarian action. The implications of this principle for the acceptance of resources are examined in greater detail in Chapter Two.

Accountability

Humanitarian organizations should report fully on their activities to sponsors and beneficiaries. Humanitarianism should be transparent.

Virtually all humanitarian agencies consider themselves accountable for the resources with which they are entrusted. UN organizations see their primary responsibility as being to member governments; donor governments, to their parliaments and taxpayers; and private agencies, to boards of directors and individual contributors. The issue is not whether the principle of accountability is important: that goes without saying. It is rather how such accountability is defined, implemented, monitored, and enforced.

Once again, an apparently self-evident principle is sufficiently complex to require careful review. The prevailing understanding of accountability is financial. Aid agencies are expected to ensure that assistance reaches those for whom it is intended, without diversion, graft, or corruption. However, conflicts inject ambiguity into such calculations. In the real world there are excruciating trade-offs between relieving suffering and ensuring accountability. Responsive action may not leave the necessary audit trail.

Can agencies assure their constituencies that during civil wars—many of them fought in countries with chronic food deficits—no food whatsoever will go to government or insurgent troops? Sometimes such assurances are indeed forthcoming. In December 1992, when U.S. troops were introduced into Somalia to protect humanitarian operations, only an estimated 10 to 20 percent of the relief food was reaching its destination. Yet one agency immediately ran full-page ads promising, "Now! All the food will reach the hungry."

T he secretary-general must commission an independent inquiry into UN famine relief. Somalia must be No. 1 on the agenda. All files must be opened, and all responsible officials summoned to testify. The proceedings must be public. Those responsible must be called to account and punished, and if necessary prosecuted. Western citizens would demand nothing less if their children were dying.
Rakiya Omaar and Alex de Waal, Africa Watch officials, 1992[8]

Accountability may require acknowledging that in such conflict settings not all food will reach those who need it, and seeking to explain why that is so. But what is an acceptable rate of "leakage" as the price for ensuring that some succor reaches civilians? Should agencies pay "protection" fees, as they did in Somalia, if the alternative is to reach fewer people or none at all? Is abetting "corruption" in the interest of avoiding starvation necessarily a bad thing? Who should make the decisions?

In modern wars, waged by citizen soldiers who are farmers one day and warriors the next, it is frequently impossible for humanitarian organizations to assure that only civilians will be helped. Providing relief supplies to women and children represents a benefit, indirect and sometimes direct, to their arms-bearing husbands and fathers. (Some women are themselves soldiers.) In fact, "humanitarian" operations located in refugee camps along the Cambodia-Thailand or Afghanistan-Pakistan borders assisted the respective war effort as an unspoken, and sometimes spoken, objective.

In the interest of accountability, what kinds of assessment and monitoring mechanisms can be expected in wars? Should normal reporting expectations be waived, or, when they cannot be satisfied, should food aid be withheld from civilians? Confronting such questions in such widely dispersed theaters as Angola and Nicaragua, Liberia and Sri Lanka, humanitarian organizations seldom have been uniform or consistent in their answers. The general experience has been, however, that the more faithful the adherence to strict standards of accountability, the more inhibited the effective relief of suffering.

Overlaying a situation in which expectations about accountability need to be approached with flexibility are pressures to apply the necessary flexibility along political lines. The U.S. government, anxious in the late 1980s to meet the needs of exiles from the violence in Nicaragua, actively sought NGOs to carry out activities along the border with Honduras. Interested agencies were promised considerable funds, freedom of action, and relaxed accountability.

When the U.S. Congress provided funds for humanitarian assistance to similar persons within Nicaragua, then under the Sandinistas, the U.S. government took an inflexible approach as to how these funds could be expended. It demanded that participating agencies assure that no funds were channeled to or through the Nicaraguan Ministry of Health or associated facilities. Thus armed conflicts may politicize not only the conduct of humanitarian operations but also accountability for those operations.

Transparency is a term increasingly introduced into discussions about improving the accountability of humanitarian responses in times of war. The logic is simple. Clear and publicly available information, particularly when combined with persistent monitoring by the media, helps assure better use of scarce resources on both the giving and the receiving ends. Debate arises, however, regarding differing conceptions of transparency and the trade-offs confronted in particular real-life situations.

From one perspective, the relief of life-threatening suffering has nothing to hide or fear from public scrutiny. In fact, transparency represents a major safeguard against the surreptitious use of aid to advance political or other hidden agendas. Humanitarian activities are the antithesis of covert action. While covert aid may benefit civilian populations, such aid fails to meet the basic tests of humanitarianism.

Yet, however compelling the principle of transparency in theory, humanitarian agencies differ on the extent to which it should be maintained at all times and in all places. Some organizations believe that had their involvement in cross-border operations into the southern Sudan or rural Liberia been more widely known, humanitarian efforts mounted within those countries from Khartoum and Monrovia might have paid a price. Saving lives, the reasoning goes, is an end in itself and should not be held hostage to the notion of openly provided assistance.

Few organizations, however, would resist the proposition that, except in highly unusual circumstances, authentic humanitarian action and transparency go hand in hand. Again, the burden should be on agencies to provide careful justifications for exceptions to the rule rather than simply to rationalize actions on the grounds that all wars are unusual and that transparency should not be expected.

Accountability, broadly viewed, requires judgment calls that range far beyond simple cost-accounting. Accountability also involves difficult programmatic trade-offs. To what extent should an agency commit the added resources required to function in settings of armed conflict? Shipments of supplies may have to go by air rather than road. Warring parties may insist that supply shipments not traverse territory controlled by their adversary. Hostilities add to insurance premiums on supplies and personnel.

In one sense, no price is too high when human lives are on the line. In another, considerations of cost-effectiveness are legitimate given limited resources and alternate uses. Agencies must determine—and be prepared to explain—to what extent the higher cost of saving lives in country *x*, at greater risk to humanitarian personnel, should be incurred rather than mounting activities in country *y*, where operations are less expensive and staff less vulnerable.

Humanitarian agencies are increasingly called to account when, soon after massive relief efforts have wound down, major food shortages recur. Why, given the global mobilization of resources for African countries during the 1984–1986 drought, were some of those same countries in need of additional assistance a few years later? To what extent should the agencies that relieve starvation be expected to help prevent similar situations from arising in the future? Difficult but legitimate questions are also asked when humanitarian assistance appears to prolong the conflicts that generated the need for such aid in the first place.

The time has come for us in the Horn of Africa to ask whether the efforts of relief agencies are contributing, indirectly or even remotely, to an escalation of the wars or to a peaceful resolution of the conflicts.
Professor Kabiru Kinyanjui, Nairobi, Kenya, 1990[9]

Even ardent supporters of United Nations peacekeeping operations question whether the presence of UN "Blue Helmets" for twenty-eight years in Cyprus may have discouraged belligerents from resolving their differences. Similarly, providers of outside assistance in war zones now question whether there are situations in which it may be preferable to stop assistance altogether. Would linking such aid to progress in negotiations be appropriate and effective?

While humanitarian or peacekeeping operations hardly can be faulted for the wars to which they are responding, they nevertheless may be expected to be more attentive to the longer-term results of their involvement. In this broader context, accountability requires the simultaneous pursuit of two objectives: to avoid sustaining the conflict that creates the need for humanitarian action, and to encourage action that serves the interests of conflict resolution and peace. The challenge is explored further in connection with the principle of contextualization later in this chapter.

Almost as difficult an issue as the nature and scope of accountability is a related matter: to whom are humanitarian organizations accountable? Traditionally, agencies have been viewed as accountable to their sources of funding. Understandable in fiscal terms, this approach has anomalous and sometimes undesirable effects. Actions by recipient governments and armed opposition groups are sometimes dictated more by the requirements of external donors than by the needs of local populations. This may moderate abuses against civilians but can also undermine the ability of local people to extract greater responsiveness from their authorities.

In recent years, growing attention has been given to the accountability of humanitarian agencies to those persons for whom their labors are intended. There is now growing consensus, although still far from unanimity, that beneficiaries should be assured roles in determining the kinds of assistance provided, in carrying out aid programs, and in evaluating their effectiveness. The implications of this principle at the operational level are explored in the discussion of mutuality in Chapter Two.

The overriding principle of all humanitarian assistance must be the recognition that ultimate accountability is to the displaced persons and not to the government, the donors or other benefactors of the humanitarian assistance programs.
U.S. Agency for International Development, 1984[10]

Appropriateness

Humanitarian action should be tailored to local circumstances and aim to enhance, not supplant, locally available resources.

While no humanitarian organizations would endorse "inappropriate" action, the concept of appropriateness involves elements that require careful analysis.

Virtually all humanitarian action involves "intervention" of one sort or another, an inflammatory concept to many. Even at a very local level when one person or community helps another, there is an element of externality. To the extent that national, regional, or international actors participate, externality is accentuated and the complexities of tailoring responses to an individual setting are heightened. As noted earlier, the degree of externality that exists in nonconflict situations is escalated when civil strife or international warfare is present. The interventionist nature of humanitarian action thus makes issues of appropriateness of great importance.

In its most fundamental sense, appropriate action involves mounting the right kinds of initiatives to benefit the right people at the right place at the right time. In some respects, however, it is easier to suggest what is appropriate by identifying what is not.

Illustrations abound. Shipments of winter clothing to hurricane victims in the Caribbean or of summer clothing to landslide victims in the Himalayas are cases in point. Distribution of foods with limited utility for religious or cultural reasons—pork for Muslims and prepackaged meals brought by U.S. troops to Ethiopians—provides other illustrations. The scale of shipments as well as their contents also can be inappropriate. The mountains of supplies rushed to Armenia following the earthquake of December 1989 now exist side-by-side with people who remain in continuing need of shelter.

Inappropriate behavior by humanitarian personnel can be equally counterproductive to effective action. Iranian media and officialdom gave considerable attention to the fact that a senior French government official's wife, accompanying a relief shipment to a camp for Iraqi Kurdish refugees in 1991, did so with her arms and head uncovered in violation of local practice. From time to time the deportment and habits, salaries, and life-styles of aid personnel themselves also become issues. On occasion, violations of law and local custom are involved.

Inappropriate inputs and behavior are regrettable in every humanitarian undertaking. When armed conflict is involved, the damage can be more serious. The arrival in mid-1991 in northern Iraq of a truck convoy carrying luxury food and clothing donated by concerned Europeans and accompanied by Western media demanded not only the immediate attention of officials on the ground but also preempted sparse warehouse space. The arrival in Somalia in 1992 of a shipment of dates, a food aid donation from a nearby Middle Eastern country, undercut international efforts to lower the value of imported relief commodities in local markets.

In situations of armed conflict, the importance of appropriate interventions is heightened. In the face of greater logistical and security challenges, diversion of time and energy can be especially unhelpful. Moreover, in politicized situations in which adversaries seek to undermine confidence in humanitarian activities, this behavior can be particularly destructive. The sexual conduct of some UN peacekeeping troops vis-à-vis the local Cambodian population in 1992 was accordingly treated with utmost seriousness by senior UN military officials. Yet time spent disciplining inappropriate behavior is time not available for other critical tasks.

Appropriateness involves not only tailoring humanitarian action to local needs, but also seeking to support indigenous capacities. Key local needs include, in addition to assisting and protecting people whose lives are threatened by war and famine, empowering individuals and institutions to fend for themselves and cope with future emergencies. Appropriate interventions build upon and strengthen individual and social coping mechanisms.

A challenge in normal circumstances, reinforcing these mechanisms is particularly difficult in armed conflicts. Disruption of local resources is sometimes an avowed objective of the warring parties. Thus, the contras targeted Nicaragua's economic and agricultural infrastructure, and the Mengistu government focused on the harvests and market towns of Tigray and Eritrea.

In a perfect world, there would be no trade-offs between saving as many lives as possible and strengthening the ability of local people and their institutions to cope more adequately with disasters. Of course, a perfect world would also be one without conflicts, famines, and the resulting need for lifesaving ministrations.

In the real world, there may be trade-offs between saving lives and empowering people, despite the agreement noted earlier that emergency action should be done in ways that strengthen local institutions. Saving lives is clear and immediate; empowering people is more ambiguous and long-term.

For some institutions, saving lives is an overriding priority, divorced from attention to the ways in which lifesaving activities are carried out. Commenting on an earlier draft of the handbook, one donor government official asserted that in the desperate case of Somalia, "We're rightly indifferent to people's cultural needs and to appropriateness issues."

Others counter that this indifference only perpetuates the vulnerability of populations to future disasters and their dependence on outside assistance, rendering future life-threatening suffering more likely. They even recommend elevating the concept of the sustainability of humanitarian action through the efforts of local people to the status of a principle in its own right.

Recent case studies suggest that the trade-offs may be less absolute than once thought. Research suggests that projects that enlist local populations and institutions are often more successful than those that do not do so. Moreover, attention to empowerment does not mean major delays in the speed of the initial responses. The spectrum from emergency relief to longer-term development described earlier is more interactive than is generally understood.

Faced with the tension between the relief of suffering and the need for appropriateness, individual agencies must establish what they consider the proper balance between saving lives in the short run and the long-term goal of strengthening local institutions to carry out future lifesaving work themselves. In doing this, they will need to avoid downplaying the importance of appropriateness, which makes humanitarian action simply a matter of mechanics, and avoid minimizing the need to save every possible life, which removes from humanitarian work its driving sense of urgency.

The challenge is complicated by the reality that some local customs may be inappropriate from an international standpoint. What of the distribution of international food aid in a situation in which the normal system favors men and boys over women and girls, or of teaching female literacy in a society in which only a small minority of girls are enrolled in primary schools? To what extent should maternal and child health centers provide counsel on female circumcision or, as Western health and legal professionals describe it, genital mutilation?

Moreover, some local institutions may not be appropriate operational counterparts for international organizations. Should external agencies enter into partnerships with indigenous groups that have their own political agendas or ethnic constituencies, or that are part of graft-ridden or patronage-oriented societies? Should allocations of food in a conflict be delegated to a council of local leaders who are all men, whose preference is for distribution among men (many of them soldiers), and whose loyalties are to their own families, subclans, and clans?

Clearly, the principle of appropriateness does not require that local practices at variance with evolving international standards remain unchallenged or that all local institutions or practices indiscriminately be strengthened. The humanitarian ethos is such that international actors need to proceed in a collegial rather than preemptory fashion in approaching these matters.

Contextualization

Effective humanitarian action should encompass a comprehensive view of overall needs and of the impact of interventions. Encouraging respect for human rights and addressing the underlying causes of conflicts are essential elements.

Humanitarian action in armed conflicts requires active involvement in situations of considerable complexity—military and political as well as economic and social. The causes of these conflicts are often deeply rooted, the societies in which they are played out deeply riven. The difficulties of providing humanitarian assistance and protection are multiple, the ripple effects from attempting to do so wide-ranging. In these situations, a comprehensive view of needs and of the likely impacts of intervention is indispensable.

A case in point is the traditional view of humanitarian assistance and human rights as separate domains, each the preserve of professionals functioning under distinct mandates and operating in relative isolation from each other. While some organizations such as UNHCR and ICRC have sought to preserve the necessary connections, many other agencies, whether for reasons of mandate, institutional style, or approach, have focused on one activity or the other.

Assistance activities position aid practitioners to serve as the "eyes and ears" of the international community, alerting the world to human rights abuses as they happen or threaten to happen. The presence of international aid personnel in places like the Sudan and El Salvador has also moderated or deterred human rights abuses by political and military actors, government and insurgent alike.

Local aid personnel frequently serve as the best sources of information for external assistance and protection agencies. Performing that function may place local and expatriate aid workers in very vulnerable situations. Yet some observers view the indirect effects of the presence of aid practitioners in moderating excesses and expressing international solidarity as more salutary than the direct impact of the succor they deliver.

An example from Ethiopia during the Mengistu years illustrates benefits and dangers alike. An expatriate NGO official at a feeding center in the north witnessed uniformed army personnel rounding up men who had come to pick up rations for their families. As the men were taken away and shot, the aid official was threatened on the spot by a senior army officer. If word of the incident leaked out, he and his Ethiopian counterparts would meet the same fate. While their presence did not prevent the killings, it was seen at least as a threat.

Conversely, protection activities give human rights personnel an excellent opportunity to document and communicate the need for humanitarian assistance. Human rights organizations monitoring abuses by the Guatemalan government have described in detail the plight of that nation's Indian population, forcibly relocated and in desperate need of emergency aid. Similarly, local and international human rights observers in the West Bank and Gaza have flagged the needs of the populations in the Occupied Territories for emergency and longer-term assistance.

Given these connections, humanitarian assistance and human rights protection are now viewed, conceptually and operationally, less as distinct enterprises than as two related sets of interventions within a common rubric. The dynamics of internal conflict make them more inseparable. The evolution in understanding and approach is more advanced in the field, where the practical linkages are everyday realities, than at the headquarters level. However, the connections also are addressed increasingly at the level of agency policy.

Establishing the connections between humanitarian assistance and human rights does not mean that an institution will be involved directly or publicly in both. Experience suggests that the respective activities require not only different competencies but also different styles of relationships with political authorities.

In his dealings with governments and insurgencies, Ambassador Jan Eliasson, UN Under-Secretary-General for Humanitarian Affairs, takes care to present his portfolio as limited to humanitarian assistance. Responsibility for issues of human rights, he tells authorities to their evident relief, is lodged elsewhere within the United Nations. The sensitivity of the connection, and the danger posed to aid operations, is suggested by the expulsion in mid-1992 of ICRC personnel from Iran, ostensibly for having shared information gained from their aid activities with human rights groups.

The interconnections between the need for emergency food, medical aid, and shelter and for the protection of human rights are so obvious and manifold that agencies involved in one or the other need to visualize their work in a larger context. After all, access to assistance is a fundamental human right, just as respect for basic human rights has a positive correlation with government policies that address essential human needs.

Humanitarian action also needs to be seen as associated with conflict resolution and longer-term development. Agencies that concentrate on the provision of emergency aid are reminded on a daily basis of the urgency of resolving the conflict that causes the suffering, and of the need for durable economic and social changes to make a society more self-reliant.

Recent experience in such settings as the Sudan, Sri Lanka, and El Salvador has demonstrated that the provision of aid—in fact, the negotiations with both sides necessary for its provision—have improved the climate for negotiations and provided a bridge to peacemaking. This is not to say that aid practitioners, there or elsewhere, have taken adequate advantage of the available openings.

Conversely, there is troubling evidence to suggest that aid has sometimes worsened the climate for negotiations and made peace a more distant goal. In Afghanistan's civil war, aid allocations by the West among the various mujahidin contributed to jockeying among them that continued even after the withdrawal of the Soviet Union. Moreover, favoritism in channeling aid through these groups at the expense of directing aid through Kabul made assistance an extension of the war rather than a contribution to peace.

There are other benefits from embracing a comprehensive view of the integral connections between humanitarian assistance, human rights, peace, and development. Doing so helps maintain a critical perspective on humanitarian operations themselves. Action-oriented institutions and activist staff need periodically to remind themselves, or to be reminded: "Don't just do something. Stand there!" Seeing the whole picture is also a useful corrective to moving from one crisis to the next, without taking time to distill the major lessons.

Seeing the whole picture also would require changes within agencies and mandates. Some legislation or regulations, for institutional or political reasons, prevent government agencies that provide emergency aid from addressing longer-term needs. In these situations, aid staff on the scene to save lives are discouraged from institution-building and reconstruction measures. The UN Transitional Authority in Cambodia was tasked with the repatriation of Cambodians and the rehabilitation of Cambodian life but was not allowed to engage in reconstruction or development activities.

Subsidiarity of Sovereignty

Where humanitarianism and sovereignty clash, sovereignty should defer to the relief of life-threatening suffering.

In interstate and intrastate conflicts, sovereignty and suffering frequently clash. The tension between the two is almost a given. The preferred outcome—that sovereign authorities either alleviate life-threatening suffering or grant humanitarian access to those prepared to do it—is far from the order of the day. Over the years, governments and insurgents alike have asserted sovereignty in order to dictate the terms under which humanitarian access will be provided, or to deny access altogether.

Recent events in Iraq, Somalia, and the former Yugoslavia have focused growing attention on the tension between sovereignty and humanitarian action. Recurring debates on humanitarian intervention in the UN Security Council, the UN General Assembly, and other fora have afforded governments opportunities to take a fresh look at the systemic tension and to strike a new balance between the two.

The economic structural adjustment programmes currently being implemented by the Central American governments do not provide the most propitious climate to consolidate democracy in Central America. The same victims of the upheaval and violence of the eighties are now paying the price of economic stabilization. The increasing impoverishment of the most vulnerable sectors of Central American society is an obstacle to reconciliation and their building of durable democratic structures.
Declaration by International NGOs, 1992[11]

Even though the notion is emerging that no nation has a right to starve or otherwise abuse its own people, the subsidiarity of sovereignty to humane values is normally affirmed only as a general principle and invoked only as a last resort. In a number of recent instances, creative humanitarian strategies for assisting civilians trapped in conflicts have succeeded in winning the consent of political authorities, thus avoiding the need to overrule or overpower them.

On these occasions the controlling powers have been persuaded that the claim of sovereignty implies certain unavoidable humanitarian obligations. Having asserted that the primary responsibility for seeing that human needs are met lies with a given government and only secondarily with the international community, the authorities have been obliged to meet those needs themselves. In this context, inviting outside assistance represents a responsible exercise of sovereignty.

To insist on the principle that sovereignty occupy a position subsidiary to humanitarian values may frame the issue in starker terms than is often necessary. Many developing countries, based on their experience with colonialism and imperialism, are deeply suspicious of "intervention," even on ostensibly humanitarian grounds.

At the same time, governments increasingly understand that claims of sovereignty are judged by its responsible—that is, its humane—exercise. Although considerations of humanity do not prevail in each and every circumstance, they are more preeminent today. Affirming the principle of the subsidiarity of sovereignty places the burden on any who, in a given instance, would elevate sovereignty over considerations of humanity. The exercise of state responsibility in this sense becomes an integral element in the invocation of national sovereignty.

However welcome this evolution, governments—and particularly intergovernmental organizations that consider themselves bound by member governments—remain reluctant to override sovereignty, even when it is invoked to deter humanitarian action. Many organizations view Security Council Resolution 688 as an exception rather than a precedent because it identified the life-endangering suffering of Kurds within Iraq as a threat to international peace and security that was sufficiently serious to justify the use of military force to create safe havens. The initial Security Council actions in Somalia and the former Yugoslavia supported this view, involving far less vigorous international military intervention than in northern Iraq.

Subsequent actions in both Somalia and the former Yugoslavia—in particular the U.S.-led multilateral humanitarian protection force in Operation Restore Hope in Somalia—have increased the validity of the view that a right to intervene is indeed evolving. Security Council Resolution 794 authorized for Somalia the use of "all necessary means in consultation with the Secretary-General," which has strengthened the precedent.

Taking a different approach from governments, NGOs generally are more willing to place moral imperatives over legal constraints. Many recognize the claims of sovereign political authorities only to the extent that those authorities respect humane values. Yet NGOs differ considerably among themselves about the extent to which they consider themselves bound by ground rules approved by governments. Most seek to operate within legal parameters as long as they can do so with integrity; some are willing to undertake illegal action when necessary to accomplish certain humanitarian tasks.

Under Article 2, paragraph 7 of the Charter, the United Nations shall never intervene in the domestic affairs of a Member State, either in the guise of preventive diplomacy or for a humanitarian aim, unless it has obtained consent to do so from all parties concerned.
Boutros Boutros-Ghali, UN Secretary-General, 1992[12]

Divergent views on the relative importance of respect for sovereignty—the quotations from Secretary-General Boutros Boutros-Ghali here and earlier in Chapter One themselves seem contradictory—should not obscure the growing consensus regarding the importance of situating humanitarian action in its political context. Agencies may differ on how they define "political" and how they protect their humanitarian activities from political influence and effects. More and more agencies, however, acknowledge the need to carry out the kind of contextual assessment described under the previous principle and developed in Chapter Two, if for no other reason than to keep their own activities as free from manipulation as possible.

Given the impossibility of isolating humanitarian action completely from the political sphere, a sense of realism suggests a middle ground between humanitarian naïveté, which denies all intersections with the political, and humanitarian realpolitik, which espouses the politicization of humanitarian action. In the final analysis, the development of a more effective international humanitarian regime will be speeded neither by denying political realities nor by embracing them uncritically.

In short, public and private agencies individually will have to make their own judgments regarding the nexus between humanitarian action and sovereignty. Continuing and sustained dialogue regarding the nature of the interaction would benefit the humanitarian community and the broader international public.

*T*he solution to the tension between sovereignty and humanitarian concern lies in redefining the sovereignty issue. Within the sovereignty of states, all these humanitarian concerns can be addressed.

Dr. Gazuli D'Faallah, former Sudanese prime minister, 1990[13]

These eight principles constitute a broad and emerging framework for humanitarian action. The issues considered legitimate subjects of international concern and action continue to grow. Just as the treatment of captured prisoners, slavery, and colonial relations, once taboo, are now clearly within the purview of the international community, so too the rights of civilians caught in zones of conflict are beginning to be viewed as legitimate objects of international concern and action.

As indicated at the outset, there are, of course, tensions between and among these Providence Principles. When conflicts among principles arise, some are given higher priority than others by different agencies. Other differences of interpretation will emerge in the light of pragmatic realities and operational constraints reviewed in the next chapter. Nevertheless, endorsement of these overarching principles—appropriately adapted to the circumstances by a particular agency operating in a theater of conflict—lays the groundwork for common policy guidelines, which form the subject of the following chapter.

NOTES

1. James P. Grant, *The State of the World's Children 1992* (New York: UNICEF, 1992): 26.

2. Javier Pérez de Cuéllar, "Report of the Secretary-General on a New International Humanitarian Order" (New York: United Nations, October 1985).

3. Boutros Boutros-Ghali, "Empowering the United Nations," *Foreign Affairs* 71: 5 (Winter 1992–1993): 98–99.

4. Francis M. Deng, "Protecting the Internally Displaced: A Challenge for the United Nations" (Washington, D.C.: The Brookings Institution, forthcoming 1993): 9.

5. InterAction Draft Statement on Humanitarian Assistance, in Larry Minear, *Helping People in an Age of Conflict* (New York and Washington, D.C.: InterAction, 1988): 82.

6. Ronaldo Mota Sardenberg, remarks to the General Assembly during the debate on "Strengthening the Coordination of Humanitarian Emergency Assistance of the United Nations," mimeographed speech of November 4, 1991: 3.

7. Cornelio Sommaruga, correspondence with the Humanitarianism and War Project, February 11, 1993.

8. Rakiya Omaar and Alex de Waal, "Somalia: See, the UN Relief System Doesn't Work," *International Herald Tribune*, August 28, 1992: 4.

9. Kabiru Kinyanjui in Larry Minear et al., *Humanitarianism Under Siege: A Critical Review of Operation Lifeline Sudan* (Trenton, N.J.: Red Sea Press, 1991): 125.

10. U.S. Agency for International Development, *Displaced Persons in El Salvador: An Assessment* (Washington, D.C.: USAID, 1984): 16.

11. Draft Declaration by International NGOs, "CIREFCA: An Instrument for Peace in Central America," April 1992: 1.

12. Boutros Boutros-Ghali, Remarks to the Summit of Non-Aligned Nations, Djakarta, September 1992.

13. Minear et al., *Humanitarianism Under Siege* (Trenton, N.J.: Red Sea Press, 1991): 99.

Chapter Two

Emerging Humanitarian Policy Guidelines: Toward More Effective Programs

Achieving broad agreement on overarching principles that provide a framework for humanitarian action is only the critical first step. The challenges of putting these principles into practice are formidable. In armed conflicts, respect for humanitarian values is tenuous, the plight of civilians perilous, the obstacles numerous, and the humanitarian response mechanisms multifarious. Yet principles must be translated into action if they are to be meaningful.

Recent experience confirms that humanitarian law and values do not command automatic respect, particularly in cauldrons of conflict where warring parties often sidestep their agreed obligations. "When a man has placed his own life on the line and is prepared to kill or die for a cause," observes Dr. Francis Deng, "it is difficult for him to be overly concerned about the humanitarian needs of those who have remained behind the enemy lines, especially if that would compromise the cause for which he has chosen to make the ultimate sacrifice."

As a result of the centuries-old temptation to make humanitarian imperatives subsidiary to political-military considerations, international legal obligations have been negotiated and sometimes updated to protect exposed civilian populations. There is also much recent evidence to suggest that, skillfully organized and creatively managed, humanitarian interests can become formidable forces in their own right, to be ignored or marginalized by belligerents at their peril. That experience can help guide the translation of principle into practice.

In 1989, Operation Lifeline Sudan made a historic contribution by employing creative humanitarian diplomacy to persuade the government and the insurgents that their political interests were served, and their military objectives were not compromised seriously, by respecting the right of their civilian populations to receive humanitarian assistance. The operation also facilitated the right of impartial aid agencies to have access to the civilians.

*M*any govern-
ments seem to
take a rather
relaxed view regarding
compliance with humani-
tarian norms, as if by
ratifying the [Geneva]
Conventions they had
been freed from all other
obligations. . . . But as
soon as they are directly
or indirectly involved in
an armed conflict, most
States qualify, interpret
or simply ignore the
rules of humanity, evok-
ing state interests and
sovereign prerogatives.
Political considerations
prevail over humanitar-
ian requirements and
humanitarian concerns
are used to further
political aims.
The Independent Com-
mission on International
Humanitarian Issues, 1988[1]

The life-and-death importance of access to civilians in times of war, gained by force if not by consent, has been subsequently dramatized in Somalia and the former Yugoslavia. Vigorous action in Somalia was reminiscent of efforts by the Allied Coalition to assist the imperiled population in northern Iraq in 1991. The human tragedy in the former Yugoslavia that continued throughout 1992 and into 1993 suggests a failure of humanitarian diplomacy to win and preserve effective access, in admittedly enormously complex circumstances.

Access is also a critical issue in situations in which life-threatening suffering is caused not by active international or civil war but by repression and structural violence. In 1992, the international community faced the challenge of dealing with systematic human rights violations by the Myanmar government and the resulting flight of civilians into neighboring Bangladesh. The United Nations sought to provide for the refugees and to moderate repression and thus enable their safe return. Similarly, the ongoing structural violence against the indigenous Guatemalan population, while sometimes stopping short of overt civil war, has called for creative humanitarian diplomacy on the part of the international community.

Where outright armed conflict occurs—or where less blatant but equally debilitating violence against the human rights of civilian populations exists—humanitarian institutions have a difficult time implementing principles and managing programs. Everyday challenges require special skills among humanitarian practitioners to prevent the muddling of principles and the return of inhumane practices.

Moreover, every humanitarian organization has its own competing priorities and pressures. None charts its course exclusively according to humanitarian considerations. Matters such as organizational visibility, fundraising, staff workload, and even religious bias often enter into decisionmaking. For these reasons it is also critical to examine the process by which principles are translated into activities and to place competing considerations more carefully in perspective.

This chapter thus reviews the operational challenges of planning, mounting, and maintaining effective humanitarian operations in situations of armed conflict.

The section entitled "Functional Checklist" provides a comprehensive checklist of specific programmatic functions that each agency needs to consider before, during, and after operations. Together they constitute "humanitarian terms of engagement," roughly analogous to the military terms of engagement that guide UN peacekeeping operations.

The subsequent section fleshes out these terms of engagement by delineating seven of the main ingredients of decisionmaking by individual agencies that decide to become operational in a given conflict setting. The complexity of the humanitarian fabric that emerges provides a backdrop for deliberations by practitioners.

The final section reviews a series of special programmatic considerations designed to help individual agencies tailor their operational responses to specific crises.

The progression in this chapter ranges from the more abstract and general to the more concrete and specific. In each instance, it is understood that individual agencies may attach different priorities to the identified considerations. As each wrestles with these issues, staff, governing boards, and partner institutions may become more informed about the approaches and decisions taken. The common ground that emerges as individual agencies address these issues is the subject of Chapter Three.

FUNCTIONAL CHECKLIST

As a tool for the early stages of agency decisionmaking, the following checklist may help assure that critical questions are asked. It can add perspective on new crises from lessons learned by earlier efforts. These are easily overlooked in the race to save lives and in the rush from today's to tomorrow's disaster. The use of similar checklists by assorted practitioners can foster mutual learning and facilitate interagency comparisons. A checklist can also identify elements for periodic review so that decisions can be evaluated as programs proceed and regular mid-course corrections are made.

A checklist such as the one proposed will not necessarily assure coordination and collegiality when emergency responses are mounted under pressure and sustained under duress. It may, however, provide individual organizations with a panorama of issues and tasks in a given setting and encourage the acceptance of a consciously delimited set of functions. A checklist also may help an agency situate itself on the relief-to-development spectrum and identify its comparative advantage.

A checklist can be helpful in disasters occasioned by "natural" causes. However, many of the identified generic tasks become more complex in time of war.

Identifying the Causes of the Crisis

Establishing the nature of the suffering: Is the life-threatening suffering that requires humanitarian action the result of natural causes, human decisions, or some combination thereof? If human decisions are implicated, will political and military factors in the situation make it more difficult to mount and sustain a humanitarian response? Will pinpointing the cause of the suffering as war or other political choices rather than drought or other "natural" causes be contested by the authorities?

Assessing the Severity of the Crisis

Establishing the need: What is the nature and extent of the need for humanitarian action? What is the geography of the need with respect to the areas controlled by the warring parties? Are the data reasonably reliable or do they reflect the self-interests of the authorities and the limitations imposed on access? Do the data reflect only well-documented need at the risk of understating the extent of the suffering, or do they make allowances to avoid underestimates? Have demographic variables, such as the number of female-headed households and unaccompanied minors, and the special needs of women been taken into account? Are the projections of need geared to a return to living standards preceding the crisis or, in situations of endemic poverty, to more adequate levels?

Making the needs assessment process inclusive: Will the warring parties participate in or be consulted during the assessment? Are the data confirmed by available evidence from local communities? Do assessment teams include the full range of institutional actors, including NGOs, so as to minimize the absence of consensus that has delayed action in the past? Is a mix of disciplines, including social sciences, involved? Will attempts be made to limit the number of separate assessment missions by individual organizations? Given the likelihood that the results will be used for political purposes, will all possible steps be taken to assure the most comprehensive and objective assessment?

Monitoring changes: What arrangements are being made to assure that the data will be regularly reviewed and revised to reflect the changing situation? Given the tendency for needs assessment figures and relief needs estimates to remain static, will humanitarian agencies be prepared to revise the estimates downward and reduce their activities according to new data?

Using the data: To what extent will the needs assessment data dictate the activities mounted, either by individual organizations or by the entire humanitarian community? Will activities proceed in the absence of a detailed needs assessment? How will humanitarian organizations deal with pressure from parliaments, the media, and the public for more reliable and more current data than may be available?

Planning documents predicated on comprehensive assessments are more likely to anticipate future programming constraints and programming opportunities. Assessments will also help to determine the appropriate resource mix to employ in response to the emergency as well as guide the financial planning and budgetary process.
Catholic Relief Services, 1992[2]

Negotiating a Framework

Approaching the authorities: By what name do the authorities wish to be called? Will humanitarian institutions speak of Cambodia or Kampuchea, the Sandinistas or the Nicaraguan government, Eritrea or northern Ethiopia? Will descriptions viewed as objective in some quarters, such as the Muslim fundamentalist government, the Marxist regime, the ruling junta, or the liberation movement, be objectionable elsewhere?

Establishing ground rules: Given the importance of agreement with the warring parties on ground rules for humanitarian activities, who will be charged with carrying out these negotiations? If they are UN authorities, will they act only on their own behalf? If they negotiate on behalf of others, will they have authorization? If the ICRC and NGOs make their own arrangements, will the United Nations respect the results of the other negotiations?

Clarifying host responsibilities: Are the host political authorities familiar with their obligations under international law? Are they prepared to accept and facilitate outside help, or are they more likely to obstruct it? Do the arrangements provide adequate space in which practitioners can function at local as well as national levels? Are the government and armed opposition groups providing assistance of an appropriate scale? What arrangements will be made where anarchy prevails and political authorities are absent or contested?

Involving local institutions: What has been done to enlist and assure appropriate partnership of local governmental and nongovernmental institutions? How sensitive to and affected by the conflict are they? What are their attitudes toward the people in need, including those of different political, ethnic, tribal, religious, or geographical origins? Will they become more affected over time by these factors or by changes in the political-military situation on the ground? Do they have the independence to function effectively? Have other steps been taken to minimize the extent to which external assistance is perceived as outside intervention?

Enlisting those in need: Have the beneficiaries been consulted? Have arrangements been made to maximize their involvement in the relief effort not only as recipients but also as owners and decisionmakers? Has a community-based approach to programming been taken? Have local residents beyond the "target population" also been consulted? How will efforts to assist those affected by the conflict be regarded by others in the region who may also have significant unmet needs?

Assuring confidentiality: Where human rights violations are involved and protection needs have been identified, have precautions been taken to protect the identities of those providing information or participating in its collection and analysis? Are there clear and appropriate terms under which this information may be shared among agencies, the authorities, and the public?

Encouraging a regional perspective: What has been done to understand the crisis in its regional context? Have the ripple effects on the region's populations and economies been addressed? Has the cooperation of neighboring countries been enlisted? Have regional financial, logistic, personnel, and other resources been mobilized? Will there be negative consequences from the involvement of neighboring countries?

Addressing special issues related to armed conflict: What distinctions have been made between civilian and combatant populations to assure that humanitarian resources are focused on the former? Have the necessary steps been taken to recognize the special situation of insurgents and develop arrangements that provide the desirable space for relief operations as well as encourage technical competence and accountability on the part of armed opposition groups? To underscore the nonpartisanship of humanitarian actions, will relief operations be coordinated from another location than the recipient nation's capital? Have protection and assistance needs been reviewed?

Humanitarian assistance is an active expression of mutual responsibility in the human community, a responsibility higher than that to any government, party, or policy. It is the unencumbered sharing of the means of life.
Corinne Johnson, American Friends Service Committee, 1987[3]

Mobilizing the Necessary Resources

Raising funds: How will resources be mobilized? Will there be a consolidated appeal, or will each agency approach the public and its own constituency exclusively on its own behalf? Are there common ground rules about how the needs will be presented by various aid actors? What measures have been taken to assure that recipients will not be depicted in ways they consider demeaning?

Building on assessments of the situation: To what extent will resource mobilization be guided by the needs, while avoiding both hype and understatement? Will fund-raising for war-related famine address or sidestep the connection between life-threatening suffering and political-military policies, as well as between emergency needs and rehabilitation and development? Will it address the special difficulties posed by armed conflicts? Will resources be mobilized and allocated toward strengthening local capacities?

Projecting costs realistically: Are the cost estimates for relief activities based on reasonable assumptions? Given the uncertainty and volatility of conflict situations, are projections based on optimistic or "worst-case" scenarios? Are anticipated costs comparable to those in similar settings? Can the proposed budget make better use of the resources committed? Can the same objectives be accomplished with fewer resources? Can goods and services be found more economically within the region? What are the operative assumptions about how long lifesaving activities will be required? Have longer-term needs for rehabilitation and development been considered?

Maintaining balanced resource allocations: What efforts will be made to assure a balance between resources needed for the particular emergency and for crises in other countries? Will the resources mobilized for this crisis be additional to those available for other crises, or will they be available at the expense of commitments needed elsewhere? Do the initial commitments of agencies assume short-, medium-, or long-term involvement? Will funds raised during the emergency phase be usable later when they may be more difficult to raise?

Orchestrating Humanitarian Activities

Determining priorities: Based on the assessment of needs for assistance and protection, what will be the major priorities for humanitarian action, both by the humanitarian community as a whole and by individual agencies?

Establishing a workable division of labor: Will the division of labor among the agencies be functional and/or geographic? Will UN agencies, donor governments, NGOs, and the ICRC each carry out operational activities? If so, will there be some specialization by functional capacity or geography among them? Will their comparative advantages be analyzed and respected? Will the experience of agencies in this or similar conflicts be exploited?

Coordinating relief activities: Who will coordinate on behalf of whom over whom? Is there a serviceable coordinating framework and mechanism in which all pillars—UN organizations, recipient and donor governments, NGOs, and the ICRC—participate at the international, national, and local levels? Beyond technical matters such as information sharing, have the political aspects of coordination been acknowledged and addressed? Who has the authority to rein in some activities or spur others? How will the special difficulties of dealing with multiple and competing host authorities be accommodated? How will an appropriate division of resources between and among people on various sides of the conflict be assured?

Maintaining effective coordination: What mechanisms will be used periodically to take stock of how formal and informal arrangements are functioning? What arrangements are in place on the "host" and the "guest" sides to resolve differences in views and approaches? Where differences persist, what sort of appeal process will be available?

Managing Communications

Nurturing effective relationships with the media: To what extent will relationships with the media be initiated and cultivated? How will the demand for accurate and current information on events in armed conflicts be satisfied? Given the various people involved—project staff in the field, regional personnel, and headquarters officials—how will information be processed? Will the media be assisted in interpreting data and developments in human terms?

Formulating policies toward the media: Which staff will have authority to deal with the media on what issues? Will they be encouraged or expected to keep the media appraised of developments? How will criticism of the host authorities be handled? Will a given agency speak only on its own behalf, or in more general terms?

Encouraging information flow involving the host country: Given the normal focus of agency communications on governing bodies, constituents, and world public opinion, what steps will be taken to facilitate a two-way flow of information to and from the affected people? Are local individuals, citizens groups, and governmental institutions fully informed about the nature and status of humanitarian initiatives? Is media from the country and region to be cultivated? What will be done to correct misconceptions or problems that develop? How will confidentiality, particularly as regards protection, be safeguarded?

Maintaining the trust of the international community: How will information be made available about expenditures and results? What balance will an agency strike between humanitarian hype, self-promotion, and self-criticism? Will there be candid reports of the ambiguities and trade-offs inherent in the humanitarian enterprise in wartime conditions? To what extent will organizations claim credit for improvements in the humanitarian situation and accept blame for negative changes?

Meeting the costs of information flow: How will the substantial costs of managing communications with professionalism in a conflict-laden situation be handled? How much are organizations that normally take a "no frills approach" to costs prepared to invest in information-related costs? To what extent will agency funds be invested in facilitating media access to conflict zones? Will an agency be prepared to underwrite the costs of accommodations and food for journalists in agency quarters when other arrangements are not possible?

Programming

Establishing realistic timetables: What operational targets will be set for the initial and later phases of an operation? Will these targets balance the urgency of relieving suffering against the constraints and complications likely to be encountered? Will they be realistic enough so that failure to achieve them will not discredit the program? Will the targets include, along with numerical goals regarding the numbers of people to be assisted, other goals such as training local personnel, strengthening national institutions, and networking with other humanitarian organizations? What mechanisms for mid-course adjustments in timetables will be instituted?

Laying the groundwork: As a result of the conflict, what special difficulties are expected from the host authorities in the normal start-up of operations? Will steps be taken to avoid problems regarding such matters as letters of agreement, visas for staff, foreign exchange rates and restrictions, duty-free entry for relief materiel, logistics (e.g., vehicles, fuel, and maintenance), and communications support (e.g., telephone, radio, and fax authorizations)? Is war-related currency fluctuation, whether inflation or devaluation, likely to be a factor? For agencies seeking to operate on all sides of a conflict, are the necessary arrangements with all the belligerents in place? Will agency experience in other settings (e.g., in developing an effective letter of agreement with the authorities) be relevant to a new crisis?

Anticipating negative externalities: What negative impacts are expected from the intervention? Will the scale of food imported affect local diets, preferences, or food prices during or beyond the emergency? Will international attention to the target population create antagonism with neighboring population groups? Will the assistance relieve the authorities of their own responsibilities, reinforce their power over the civilian population, and fuel or perpetuate the conflict? Will the projected number of expatriate staff have negative economic, social, or cultural impacts on the local situation? What will be done to avoid or minimize such problems?

Clarifying relations between humanitarian activities and military forces: Given the vulnerability of relief operations where insecurity prevails, to what extent will an organization seek or accept armed protection? Does the origin of a protection force (from the warring parties, local mercenaries, an outside government, a regional intergovernmental body, or the United Nations) have a bearing on its acceptability? Will an agency allow humanitarian relief supplies to be transported in convoys that contain nonhumanitarian items? Will military transport be used for civilian humanitarian personnel, or vice versa?

Balancing operational and other concerns: What precautions will be taken to counteract the natural tendency for logistical concerns to become an all-consuming preoccupation? What steps will be taken to assure that relief operations proceed in tandem with other important activities, such as information flow, networking with other aid agencies, liaison with host authorities, protection of civilian populations, and attention to longer-term development?

Identifying linkages along the relief-to-development spectrum: Will the early stages of responses to life-and-death emergencies be exempted from an obligation to future-oriented approaches? How will a specific intervention capitalize on recent experience that suggests that development-oriented relief interventions can be more successful in short- as well as longer-term perspectives? What will be done to integrate into the concept of "humanitarian action" such activities as constructing health clinics, training schoolteachers, and organizing local communities?

Establishing connections between assistance and protection concerns: Given the normal division of labor between humanitarian assistance and human rights agencies, what measures will be taken to reflect the linkages between aid and protection issues? Will the "eyes and ears" function of aid personnel be placed officially or informally at the service of groups whose primary function is protection? Conversely, will the strategies of human rights groups and the information they amass be communicated appropriately to their aid counterparts? What ground rules will be established regarding information-sharing and what safeguards regarding confidentiality? Will the special protection needs of vulnerable groups (for example, the disabled, children, and women) be taken into account in assistance projects? Will assistance strategies render those who have been helped less susceptible to protection problems? Will appropriate distinctions be made between responsibilities for human rights monitoring and protection activities themselves?

Promoting synergisms between aid provision and conflict resolution: In view of successful international assistance in moderating conflict, supporting political accommodation, and encouraging a durable peace in some situations, what will be the relation between outside aid and efforts to mitigate conflict or foster negotiations? Given the possible confusion of roles that may result when assistance agencies exceed their mandates and competence, what steps will be taken to support the efforts of other organizations to enable reconciliation and political solutions?

Staffing Humanitarian Operations

Enlisting appropriate personnel: How will the necessary international personnel be quickly identified and deployed? How will persons with prior knowledge of and experience in the country or region be pressed into service? How will persons with competence in conflict situations be enlisted—such as those who can manage difficult relationships with uncooperative political authorities, deal with the media sensitively on controversial subjects, and function well under stress? Will special arrangements be made for insurance, home leave, and nonaccompanying family members?

Using existing national and regional personnel: How will efforts be maximized to enlist qualified staff from the country and the region? Will the operation involve national and regional staff at all levels of responsibility?

Will women be given appropriate positions of authority? What responsibilities will the employing agencies assume for the security of national staff and their families who, once identified with a controversial humanitarian initiative, may be in jeopardy?

Providing the necessary training: What steps will be taken to assure that all personnel—international, regional, and national—are properly oriented to the conflict and the cultural setting in which they must function and to their responsibilities? How will the difficulty of providing training in the midst of a crisis be addressed? Will training be made available on matters of human rights, humanitarian law, and gender-sensitivity?

Assuring the necessary security: What precautions will be taken to minimize the risks involved in deploying humanitarian personnel in emergency situations? What types of mechanisms will be used to provide day-to-day protection for staff engaged in assistance and protection activities, particularly those drawn from the nations or areas in turmoil, who are vulnerable to pressure from authorities? What will be the criteria determining whether to deploy personnel in a war zone? What evacuation procedures will be followed? What will be the ground rules for staff carrying weapons, and for relief supplies and agency property being protected by weapons? Will the added costs of protection be considered legitimate agency expenditures?

Meeting the psychological needs of staff: Given the heightened stress of emergency relief operations in conflicts, what provisions will be made before deployment to identify persons capable of handling stress well? Will additional personnel be posted to take on the more complex tasks? What arrangements will be made to provide necessary support and periodic rests?

We're supposed to be here on a humanitarian mission, and yet we're getting shot at. It's very confusing.
U.S. Marine in Somalia, 1993[4]

Assuring Accountability

Clarifying expectations: What accountability will be required of humanitarian personnel and aid organizations? How regular and detailed will be the reports? Will expectations be tailored according to the exigencies of the particular conflict? What will be considered acceptable levels of "leakage" and reasonable payments for security? Will the same procedures and forms be used for activities on all sides of the conflict? Who will report to whom?

Taking special factors into account: Will normal reporting expectations be relaxed or waived in the interest of quicker delivery of relief supplies? For how long a period? Will special precautions be taken to monitor the potential diversion of relief supplies to combatants or prohibitions against access by belligerents? Will reports from personnel on each side of the conflict be consolidated as part of a single program or will separate programs be maintained?

With this checklist in hand, the governing boards, senior executives, and field personnel can review and determine the humanitarian terms of engagement for their institution in an emergency operation. Attention now turns to the matter of deciding whether, when, and how to engage in a particular theater of operations.

INSTITUTIONAL BENCHMARKS FOR ACTION

There are seven institutional benchmarks from the preceding functional checklist that may help organizations establish a more specific rationale for taking action. Examples drawn from field research of the Humanitarianism and War Project illustrate central elements in decisionmaking responses to a particular emergency.

Individual agencies will attach their own significance and priority to each of the following considerations. For some, a given element or a combination of elements may constitute a precondition for involvement in a life-threatening emergency; for others, the same benchmark may represent a desirable but not indispensable trigger for action. While various organizations may view the importance of individual benchmarks differently, each benchmark affects them all.

This section reviews criteria for decisions about whether to undertake, sustain, or withdraw from a particular humanitarian operation. The process of determining the humanitarian terms of engagement for a specific crisis involves establishing the importance of various benchmarks at the *intra*-agency level. The elements identified below also may serve to facilitate *inter*agency discussions about overcoming common problems.

Contextual Analysis

Recent experience in providing assistance and protection in armed conflicts demonstrates a positive correlation between a thorough understanding of the contexts of suffering and effective efforts to respond. For all their idiosyncrasies, conflicts in countries as disparate as Somalia and Sri Lanka, Cambodia and Guatemala, Iraq and Liberia, and Afghanistan and the former Yugoslavia exhibit common interactions between human needs and humanitarian responses on the one hand, and broader political, economic, and military realities on the other. Thus the first benchmark in institutional decisionmaking involves contextual analysis and comprises four issues.

First, although frequently unacknowledged by decisionmakers within humanitarian agencies, many exigencies arising in emergency situations have their roots in underlying political, economic, and military realities. Several years ago, the Bellagio Declaration observed that because technological breakthroughs make it increasingly possible to eradicate famine-associated mortality in situations where civil strife is not present, "the major obstacle to eliminating famine remains the destruction or interdiction of civilian food supplies in zones of armed conflict."

When the African drought of the mid-1980s finally subsided, human suffering continued unabated in Angola, Mozambique, Ethiopia, and the Sudan. What linked these countries then was no longer drought but civil strife. More recently, warfare has compounded and sustained the ravages of nature in Angola, Mozambique, and Somalia. In many other areas, too, vulnerability to recurrent famine has gone hand in hand with chronic underdevelopment. Haiti and Bangladesh, among the world's poorest countries, have been among the nations least able to protect themselves against disasters.

Second, conflict is now a major culprit in creating the world's "internally displaced persons," who now greatly outnumber "refugees." This distinction is more than semantic: the benefits of international assistance and protection programs are directly linked to whether a person enjoys recognized refugee status by virtue of having crossed an international border or is displaced within a country of origin.

In Africa today millions of people have been uprooted from their homes because of civil and ethnic conflict, human rights abuses, and the famine and suffering that accompany these shattering events. . . . Resolving these root causes sometimes produces other categories of uprooted people: demobilized soldiers and returning refugees, many of whom find it difficult to reintegrate into their home communities.
Refugee Policy Group, 1992[5]

However arcane such distinctions may appear to the uninitiated, they are a major concern for officials within agencies like UNHCR and the ICRC that concentrate on protection. There is considerable flux in today's world. For example, Serbs and Muslims in Croatia became "refugees" after Croatia was recognized officially as an independent state. Operational issues are rarely separated from international norms, however arbitrary. Consequently, UNHCR had little choice but to play the role of lead agency in the area, even before many internally displaced persons technically became refugees.

On the more positive side, some observers have noted a connection between protecting human rights and avoiding social upheaval and human displacement. Democratic traditions distinguish Costa Rica, which was spared civil strife during the 1980s, from El Salvador and Guatemala, which lacked mechanisms for encouraging broad popular participation. The restoration of a free press in the Sudan would represent an important step toward the establishment of more humane government policies toward its citizens, including an end to war and war-related famine.

Third, the role of military force in exacerbating or alleviating human needs also emerges as a now-major issue that requires further analysis. On the negative side, the use of military force and military personnel in a variety of theaters has created a wide array of humanitarian problems. The jury is still out on the longer-term impacts of using military force in humanitarian problem-solving.

At the same time, there have been several recent instances in which the application of military force has been constructive, at least in the short term. Northern Iraq and Somalia come to mind, as does Liberia. In the latter instance, the application of military force by the Economic Community of West African States (ECOWAS) appears to have provided elements of stability in specific areas that facilitated the relief of human need.

At a time when the UN Security Council deepens its involvement in addressing major humanitarian emergencies through economic and military sanctions, humanitarian institutions working in conflicts are challenged to articulate their views of the legitimacy and appropriateness of using coercion or of being associated with its use.

Are these organizations prepared to subject their relief shipments to review by a UN sanctions committee or to inspection by military authorities? Are they ready to provide assistance within protected enclaves secured by military force? Will they be willing to carry out humanitarian work under a UN umbrella, responding to needs generated by a war pursued in response to the resolutions of its Security Council? Will they allow their relief convoys to be accompanied by military contingents and their personnel to be protected by armed bodyguards? Under what circumstances are personnel to be committed to or withdrawn from areas of armed conflict? Does association with outside military forces help or hinder future access once the troops have departed?

These are troublesome questions requiring answers, even by organizations operating in crises yet unaddressed by Security Council action. Although it may be difficult to establish answers that are "right" in any prescriptive sense for the humanitarian community as a whole, it is necessary to find a proper fit between individual agencies and particular approaches. In the current post–Cold War moment, the timeworn reflexes of agencies, either to embrace or dismiss one approach or the other, require reconsideration.

Agencies for which the utilization of economic or military force traditionally has been antithetical to the pursuit of humanitarian objectives now need to think seriously about the consequences of their refusal to become operational in these situations. There are some instances in which, without protection greater than moral suasion, personnel cannot function. Conversely, agencies for which coercion typically has raised no insuperable ethical issues now need to consider whether durable benefits to vulnerable populations can be sustained when access is assured only under duress.

Fourth, there are clear—if complex—linkages among conflict, underdevelopment, coercion, and human rights abuses. More positively, there are interactions among humanitarian assistance, the resolution of conflicts, and the realization of these rights as food, development, and peace.

Based on analyses of many regions in conflict, the Humanitarianism and War Project concludes that agencies specializing in one particular area should become more catholic in their concerns, even if their own projects and programs retain a more specialized focus. As noted earlier, the presence of external organizations provides a protection as well as an assistance function. The "eyes and ears" of emergency aid personnel can be helpful in reporting infringements on human rights as well as in suggesting ideas for future reconstruction and development projects. The collaboration of belligerents on relief also opens up the possibility of movement toward peace.

There is a sort of circle here. Development cannot be achieved without peace; without development, human rights are illusory; and peace without human rights is violence.
Reginald Moreels, president of Médicins Sans Frontières–Belgium, 1989[6]

Although the Sudan case study encouraged organizations to remain on the scene but to broaden their horizons, subsequent developments in April 1992 led the United Nations to suspend relief operations in the Sudan because they lacked the necessary space within which to function effectively. During 1992, eleven humanitarian aid personnel are understood to have died in the Sudan. The death toll was probably higher in Somalia.

Additional research in Africa, Asia, Latin America, and Europe also suggests that however desperately needed humanitarian activities may be, there should be no automatic presumption in favor of involvement. Moreover, there is no particular wisdom for an agency, once involved, to remain when circumstances make relief activities nonproductive or even counterproductive. While all possible alternative strategies should be explored, the decision to abandon a particular humanitarian terrain may be the best approach in the worst case.

Again, there will be significant differences among actors. UN agencies may be more obliged to become involved in every major crisis than donor governments or NGOs. As the situation in Somalia and Liberia demonstrated, they may also be absent unless donor governments or public pressure demand their presence. NGOs are generally less stringent in their security requirements and tend to tackle some of the more perilous challenges. As a matter of principle and practice, the ICRC places a higher premium to remain on the scene and, when it finally decides to leave (as in Somalia in 1991), returns at the earliest possible opportunity.

In short, contextual analysis requires finely tuned judgments by individual organizations based on details of specific conflicts. Having studied the lay of the land, some institutions may decide not to become operationally involved. For many agencies, however, whose raison d'être is to provide assistance and protection, not to act verges on the unthinkable.

Recent experience indicates that agencies are advised to look carefully before they leap into action. While many concede that there may be circumstances in which they cannot carry out programs with integrity, few recall instances in which they have refused to initiate operations or have suspended programs already under way. Unwillingness to identify the elements which would lead them to say "no" to alleviating suffering implies that they are so committed to their mission that they will proceed regardless of the circumstances.

It is also true that deferring humanitarian action has consequences. Persons already in need of assistance suffer a second indignity when humanitarian agencies concede that they cannot be reached in whatever the circumstances. Deferred action represents a setback for humanitarian organizations, both for their own mission and for their public identification with effective action. The decision to opt out also surrenders an organization's place at the table where host authorities can be influenced to adopt more humane policies.

From a humanitarian standpoint, some reasons for deferring action are more appropriate than others. If activities cannot be protected from abuse or project personnel from harm, a decision to defer makes sense. Withholding aid as a bargaining chip to extract concessions might compromise the integrity of humanitarian action. It would concede to the authorities the power to prohibit humanitarian access and undercut the principle of relieving suffering and that of proportionality.

Division of Labor

The presence of hundreds of aid organizations and thousands of aid personnel in major emergencies makes it essential to address their respective comparative advantages, particularly when armed conflict complicates aid efforts. Doing this is particularly important in the post–Cold War era, when conventional notions about agency roles are questioned.

In fact, a greater tolerance of ambiguity and messiness is required by the new and untidy world with a multiplicity of actors, which defies efforts to devise models suitable for every situation. New interactions that combine universal and regional, public and private, governmental and nongovernmental elements—and perhaps also new institutions—are the order of the new day.

The functional checklist detailed at the beginning of this chapter is an appropriate point of departure for determining whether an agency is in a position to make an essential contribution in a conflict and, if so, what is its comparative advantage. The checklist identifies functions that need attention, whether or not an individual agency undertakes all of them. For purposes of illustration, the functions of needs assessment, coordination, and programming will be examined.

• *Needs assessment:* Although each organization is not required to gather detailed data for its own assessment of the severity of a crisis, a realistic picture of the need is indispensable for effective action. But which organizations are best suited to carry out needs assessments? The answer depends on the situation.

While the United Nations is assumed to enjoy a comparative advantage, recent experience in the Horn of Africa suggests that the UN's exclusion from areas not under government control may undermine the utility of its figures. Thus OLS activities, based initially on data hastily assembled by UN officials in Khartoum without access to insurgent-held areas, eventually led to serious operational difficulties.

In the civil conflicts in Central America, UN organizations and personnel occasionally have gained access to contested areas from which NGOs have been barred. This suggests that the needs assessment function may be one in which a combination of official and unofficial approaches provides the best basis for programming decisions. Yet that would require far greater collegiality among humanitarian organizations than often exists.

• *Coordination:* It is taken for granted that the United Nations should assume coordinating responsibilities in every major crisis. Experience suggests that the UN system's bias toward governments—it is an *intergovernmental* organization—creates difficulties in dealing with insurgencies, even on humanitarian grounds. Here, too, there may be differences among UN organizations. UNHCR in some African crises, but not in other Central American ones, has proved more able to deal evenhandedly with insurgents and governments.

The structural bias of many UN organizations creates problems in their dealings with NGOs, many of which seek to maintain distance from governments. In the interest of evenhanded coordination, alternative arrangements have been devised. With the United Nations unwelcome in Ethiopia in the mid-1980s, national NGOs established the Joint Relief Partnership, which successfully negotiated with the government in Addis Ababa and the Tigrayan People's Liberation Front to provide assistance to Tigray and northern Shewa.

• *Programming:* Because they frequently enjoy close working relationships with communities most directly affected by armed conflict, it is assumed that NGOs should concentrate on the delivery of relief assistance. Yet NGOs may also help bridge gaps between warring parties and facilitate negotiated settlements. The World Council of Churches and the All

Africa Conference of Churches brokered the Addis Ababa Accords of 1972, which halted the Sudan's seventeen-year civil war. The current humanitarian crisis in Somalia, in which the United Nations only late in the tragedy made a serious attempt to resolve the conflict, also witnessed promising NGO initiatives.

Each of the respective organizational actors that compose the present international humanitarian system was created at a historical moment for specific purposes. Over time, most have assumed additional tasks and expanded their mandates. The end of the Cold War and the upsurge of humanitarian demands makes the present moment propitious to reexamine the international division of humanitarian labor to maximize strengths and offset weaknesses.

In that context, the following questions may help individual agencies identify their actual or potential comparative advantages:

1. Have we accumulated specific expertise (for example, in a specific sector [such as food distribution or emergency medical services], geographical region [such as Southern Asia], or linguistic area [such as Central America or Francophone Africa])?
2. Have we developed program support mechanisms that could be useful in a given region (such as the Horn of Africa) or for a particular program (such as food transport or human rights reporting)?
3. Do we have familiarity with affected population groups (such as refugees or internally displaced persons, unaccompanied minors, street children, or soldiers in need of demobilization)?
4. Does the makeup of our institution and our staff position us to respond (for example, as a secular agency to a crisis with religious overtones, or with personnel from nonaligned country backgrounds in an emergency with geopolitical dimensions)?
5. Do we have natural affinities or previous working relationships with indigenous partner agencies (for example, a Red Crescent society, a church or group of churches, a professional association of nutritionists, or government disaster specialists) that are in a position to make contributions?
6. Are we able to mount programs quickly through redeploying staff, advancing resources, and expediting relief materiel, or are we better suited to make a contribution later?
7. Do we have the requisite familiarity with international humanitarian law and human rights law, including refugee law, for situations in which gaining and maintaining access for assistance and protection personnel to those in need may be difficult?
8. Are we prepared to take risks (such as deploying personnel in situations of insecurity and providing the necessary backup support)?

9. Are we able and willing to handle controversies likely to develop in situations in which competing political authorities or repressive governments may challenge humanitarian activities, and in which normal accountability expectations are difficult to fulfill?

Resources

As noted in the discussion on accountability, the cost of carrying out effective programs in armed conflicts is high. In Operation Lifeline Sudan, aid agency expenditures in many budget lines were swollen by what was essentially a "war tax." For example, transport costs and insurance were higher because of the war. This also drove up personnel costs because more intensive monitoring was necessary to prevent abuse. The war taxes were more visible and higher still in Somalia, where aid agencies routinely paid tens of thousands of dollars per month for "protection" by local "technicals."

While precise data are sketchy, this general pattern also holds elsewhere. It is more expensive to function in civil wars than in nonconflict-related emergencies or in reconstruction or development contexts. Costs escalate not only because logistics and personnel are more expensive but also because the noncooperation of belligerents often results in expensive interruptions in delivery.

Public interest generated in a major emergency—for example, in the Ethiopian famine by the British Broadcasting Corporation exposé in October 1984—usually ensures a substantial (or even an overwhelming) tranche of resources. At these times, the UN makes special appeals, parliaments pass special appropriations, NGOs open special accounts, and major programs then may be launched.

On the other hand, the politics of a particular crisis may make mobilization of resources easier even if the magnitude of the emergency is small. Hence, NGOs were able to mount and sustain significant efforts in Central America in the 1980s for numbers of refugees and internally displaced persons that were modest in comparison with civilian suffering flowing at that time from wars in Afghanistan or Mozambique.

Experience suggests that an initial upsurge in donor interest should be treated cautiously. First, as the media move on to other subjects, contributions plateau and then decrease, requiring reduced activities later unless anticipated from the start. Resource commitments over the years often have been more generous during the emergency phase of a disaster than during subsequent rehabilitation, medium-term reconstruction, and development phases. Current donor lethargy or tardiness in underwriting the costs of post-conflict reconstruction and peacekeeping in many former Cold War hot spots provides a poignant case in point.

Second, public interest is frequently "behind the curve." An emergency often will be well advanced and more expensive to address when it becomes a matter of international concern. By the time television news pictured Ethiopians trekking to relief camps in late 1984, many persons had already died. The modest investments that might have served the cause of famine prevention were upstaged by the need for more massive commitments for famine alleviation.

Third, legislation in some donor countries specifically prohibits anything other than emergency humanitarian assistance to "pariah" states. By allowing aid directed only toward the immediate saving of lives, countries thwart preventive measures against future disasters. Agencies committed to longer involvement would be advised to assess the political lay of the land before mounting emergency programs with restricted funds.

Experience also indicates that there are high costs in responding quickly to new conflicts. UN and government agencies, NGOs, and the ICRC all responded to the crisis in the former Yugoslavia by shifting seasoned personnel from other duty stations. Robbing Peter may be helpful to Paul, but it can reverse momentum in troubled areas that had taken years to establish. Agencies need to count the indirect as well as the direct costs of mounting and sustaining effective new emergency programs.

If continuity of resources for conflict-related humanitarian work is a problem, so too is the nature of the resources available. This applies particularly to NGOs. Some, such as the American Friends Service Committee, accept no resources from governments on the grounds that their freedom of action and rationale for responding will be compromised. Others, such as CARE, generally accept whatever resources are offered, once they have assured themselves that they have not compromised their independence and desire to enhance their ability to respond. Still others, such as Save the Children–UK, take into account the resources offered by a particular government or UN agency for selected purposes in identified countries.

There are also differences in the perceived appropriateness of resources that depend on the individual UN organizations that offer them. The ICRC receives 90 percent of its budget each year from government funds, but it has worked hard to protect its well-recognized independence.

The source of funds obviously matters. During the Cold War, the availability of resources from the U.S. government confronted U.S. NGOs with more difficult choices than those faced by Canadian or Dutch NGOs, which were offered resources by their governments. U.S. NGOs were also under pressure to accept these funds because of public and congressional distrust of aid channeled on a government-to-government basis. However, U.S. funds were not the only ones made available to advance particular political agendas. In a broader view, funds from every government deserve critical scrutiny, even in the post–Cold War era.

U.S. NGOs reviewed these issues during the three-year series of discussions mentioned earlier. They concluded that those NGOs that test their

*H*umanitarian
*. . . assistance
does not validate or invalidate itself
by virtue of its relation,
positive or negative, to
U.S. foreign policy. Humanitarian assistance
does not become authentic simply by virtue of
being called humanitarian, whether by the U.S.
government or U.S. private organizations. It
distinguishes itself instead by its effective and
accountable responsiveness to critical human
needs, wherever people
are suffering.*
Larry Minear, codirector,
Humanitarianism and War
Project, 1988[7]

humanitarian assistance, whether or not it is compatible with U.S. foreign policy, may have difficulty explaining how the aid can follow the flag and still meet international expectations of impartiality. On the other hand, those maintaining that their aid is humanitarian just because it goes where the U.S. flag does not may be hard-pressed to explain their lack of responsiveness to the urgent needs of persons who happen to be located in countries of particular interest to the U.S. government.

The end of the Cold War does not magically guarantee that funds available from governments or intergovernmental organizations for humanitarian purposes will be without strings attached. Although multilateral approaches to problem solving have a greater following in the aftermath of the Cold War, the experience of UN agencies and associated NGOs in Iraq provides a reminder that resources provided in a highly politicized context may appear suspect to those for whom they are intended. A blue flag does not better guarantee apolitical humanitarianism than a red, white, and blue one.

In sum, the high costs of functioning in conflicts should inject caution as agencies project likely resource needs. Prudence dictates a view that is both realistic about the difficulty of sustaining contributions and wary of the overt or hidden agendas that often accompany resources.

Mutuality

This fourth institutional benchmark deals with growing pressures to create productive partnerships between external and indigenous individuals and organizations.

In recent years, developing countries have insisted on playing a more decisive role in the planning and management of humanitarian activities. Many international aid institutions and officials have affirmed the importance of encouraging greater host-country participation, even though there has been great unevenness in relations between external actors and their partners at national and local levels in the affected countries.

Partnership in humanitarian action, however attractive and even axiomatic on its face, involves troublesome issues. In armed conflicts where lives are on the line, practitioners frequently confront what they perceive as a direct trade-off between responding quickly to an emergency and using that response for local capacity-building purposes.

As indicated earlier, the problem is less that of an either/or choice than of a continuum of options. What matters most is the effective identification of local capacity and its maximum use, strengthening it when possible but also supplementing it with outside capacity to the extent that local resources are inadequate to the task. There will be times and places when major and swift involvement by outside organizations is indispensable although with the caveat that opportunities to use local resources must be sought constantly.

The dilemma is highlighted by interviews with practitioners in war-torn areas. Although most institutions agree on the importance of capacitation, they give an even higher priority to quick response, which usually means shouldering the work themselves rather than taking the time to explore alternatives. Local organizations, for the most part ignored in the process, offer a bridge between activities that are heavily external and Western in nature and indigenous institutions and people.

All external aid agencies should invest more resources and resourcefulness into capacity-building. If this were a major operational objective, indigenous institutions often could be strengthened without slowing the pace of relief activities. This approach would have left Angola and Cambodia better positioned to meet future emergencies and eventually to undertake reconstruction and development challenges. Investments in early warning also would prepare the institutions to assume larger roles when crises occur.

Mutuality poses other difficulties for humanitarian organizations. External agencies are increasingly known by the company they keep, so the selection of counterparts becomes critical. Identifying compatible and effective partners is difficult: local counterparts may be weak, ineffective, scarce, or politicized. While "indigenous" organizations can be created from the outside to make up for the lack of appropriate counterparts, doing so raises issues regarding the authenticity, independence, and capacity-building potential of such constructs.

The search for partners sometimes creates inappropriate bedfellows. One major international NGO claimed that its activities in insurgent-controlled areas of the southern Sudan were nonpartisan despite carrying out its program through an NGO—in this instance, international—that had publicly endorsed the insurgents' cause. The *International* Committee of the Red Cross, which places a premium on maintaining independence from governments, also keeps under review its relationships with *national* Red Cross and Red Crescent societies, which sometimes lack independence.

Once partners are identified, nurturing mutual relationships can be laborious. External agencies generally wish to see their resources disbursed as quickly as possible for activities that directly benefit the needy.

The partnership principle entails concerted decisions by NGOs and UNHCR throughout the entire cycle of programme planning and implementation. Joint needs assessments lead to the formulation of policy guidelines, project objectives and design. NGOs can contribute their special knowledge of local conditions. NGOs recognize the need for UNHCR to monitor the use of funds and other resources allocated to them and to coordinate programmes effectively.
International Council of Voluntary Agencies and UNHCR, 1992[8]

Indigenous organizations may give priority instead to long-term efforts, bricks-and-mortar, or administrative items. International organizations tend to seek identifiable projects; indigenous partners may prefer budget support or programming that consolidates funds from many sources. The promotional needs of external donors often run afoul of the sensitivities of local partners.

There also may be tensions of accountability. Donors insist that partners be accountable to them, while indigenous organizations see themselves as accountable to their constituencies. In fact, the traditional categories of "donor" and "recipient" do violence to the concept of mutuality by reinforcing the stereotype that accountability is a one-way street.

Despite the difficulties, there are clear benefits in mutuality and capacity-building. Mutuality reduces the foreign element in relief interventions and builds for the future by strengthening indigenous leadership and institutions. The high cost of international personnel and materiel, and the potential cost-effectiveness of expenditures on local human and material resources, make mutuality economically appealing.

Education

Agencies differ widely in their approach to the functions of education and advocacy. Despite considerable lack of agreement on how these functions should be approached, their importance requires their inclusion as the fifth and sixth benchmarks in intra-agency decisionmaking on humanitarian action.

To what extent do agencies have an obligation to educate their constituencies about the causes of human suffering? All agencies have programs designed to provide public information about their activities. Educational efforts are viewed as a means to nurture ongoing support and mobilize resources and as necessary elements of accountability. They also may provide the basis for affirming mutuality and for capacity-building.

Differences in how agencies define and approach education range from providing information to changing prevailing attitudes. Some agencies limit informational activities to descriptions of their projects. Some set their projects in the context of the broader needs of a community or society. Some take a wider view and establish connections between policies of developing country governments and their people. Some are global in their approach, connecting the policies of industrialized nations to human needs in developing countries.

Some organizations, particularly church-related NGOs dedicated to social justice and secular groups such as Oxfam, see extensive educational activities as part of their core mandates. Some give preference to projects that have special educational potential for publics in industrialized countries. Others stress the delivery of humanitarian services without an educational component that transcends the description of project activities.

If there are variations in how the education task is framed, there are also differing approaches as to how it is conducted. Some agencies, such as UNICEF, have large budgets for public information that underwrite goodwill ambassadors and tours of journalists. Some governments—the Nordics and Canadians in particular—provide public funds to NGOs for development education. The Biden-Pell grants of USAID underwrite an array of educational efforts by U.S. NGOs and civic groups.

The ICRC carries out extensive "dissemination" activities each year, including seminars for diplomats and public officials on international humanitarian law. UNHCR's educational activities include refugee law training for government officials (particularly in the determination of refugee status) and for NGO partners, all within a human rights law context.

Not all agencies committed to attitudinal changes in the industrialized world mount their own educational initiatives. Some support activities carried out by consortia or individual organizations on behalf of the wider community. Other agencies undertake an array of educational initiatives: for example, at the global level, the Geneva-based International Council of Voluntary Agencies, with a membership of 89 organizations or groups of organizations; and in individual countries, associations like the Washington-based InterAction, with 140–plus individual agencies as members.

A collective approach has proved advantageous in maximizing educational impact. Criticism of the arms export policies of Germany or France, for example, may be taken more seriously when it comes from a coalition of agencies instead of from a single group. A joint initiative also provides protective cover for agencies taking controversial stands—for example, those who critique the impact of Northern consumption that is patterned on Southern societies.

Agencies also differ on whether educational activities are considered a program or an administrative expense. This is an especially sensitive matter for NGOs, which are frequently judged according to the percentage of funds that directly reach the suffering. Treated as an administrative charge, educational expenditures inflate overhead costs. Many agencies therefore either keep these expenditures to a minimum or treat them as a program expense. However paid for, effective educational activities require a professionalism and long-term commitment that some agencies are hard-pressed to honor.

Advocacy

If education is geared toward informing and changing public views on the nature and causes of life-threatening suffering, advocacy activities are designed to change the policies of governments in developing and developed countries. Here, too, agencies view advocacy and chart their courses differently. The basic question concerns the extent to which they have an obligation to address government policies and policymakers with an eye to changing the status quo.

A recent retrospective among Addis-based NGOs of their relations with the Mengistu regime concluded that with the benefit of hindsight, a number of agencies would have chosen to be bolder—but not much—in challenging the policies of the Ethiopian government during the 1980s. Had they been more outspoken, they believe, they might have found themselves expelled by the Mengistu government, as were (on different occasions) Médecins Sans Frontières and the ICRC. Expulsion forecloses any opportunity to provide further direct humanitarian assistance, whatever positive value the policy change or public relations impact of an agency's departure may have. At the same time, such groups as Cultural Survival and Africa Watch rightly ask whether sharper criticism early on could have prevented massive human suffering later.

Agencies that do not seek to change government policies may have an easier time pursuing humanitarian aid activities in their own right. Yet they expose themselves to criticism for having applied "Band-Aids" to systemic problems, and for ostensibly consigning their beneficiaries to recurrent hardships. Thus agencies helping persons forcibly relocated by governments in such places as Ethiopia, the Sudan, El Salvador, and Guatemala—by not simultaneously challenging those policies—have been criticized for contributing indirectly to these inhumane practices.

Changing the policies of governments frequently has been viewed as the special province of NGOs, and then of only the most "radical" among them. But individual donor governments have also pressured belligerent authorities for policy changes that would expand access to civilian populations and reduce abuses. Ambassadors of these governments have met with political authorities in the capitals of conflict-ridden countries to escalate pressure. Sometimes national legislation in donor countries requires policy changes on the receiving end in order to continue assistance.

Some intergovernmental agencies also have made it their business to challenge the policies of governments or of other UN organizations. In 1990, UNICEF highlighted the negative effects of structural adjustment urged by the World Bank and the International Monetary Fund on low-income populations throughout the developing world. More recently, UNICEF and some NGOs also have criticized the effects of the sanctions imposed by the UN Security Council on Iraq, Haiti, and the former Yugoslavia. In 1991, the World Food Programme appealed to the UN Sanctions Committee to relax its policies regarding Iraq. On various occasions, UNHCR has challenged governments and other parts of the United Nations perceived as interfering with the implementation of its mandate.

As in education, there are potential trade-offs between hard-hitting or even low-key advocacy and continued operational cooperation with governments. Even though it also strongly challenges government policies that create major humanitarian problems, the ICRC cautions against seeking "to help and to condemn in the same country." External and indigenous organizations obviously face different risks and costs in pursuing advocacy.

At the same time, however, changes in the international division of labor are making public policy advocacy more feasible. Southern NGOs are encouraging Northern colleagues to focus less on operational activities in the South and more on attitudes and policies in the North. Northern NGOs increasingly are directing their advocacy efforts at Northern governments, while Southern NGOs are targeting their own authorities.

This arrangement is not without problems. Criticism may be more acceptable to developing country governments when it comes from indigenous institutions; however, such criticism is easier to discourage or suppress. And although Northern NGOs have better access to Northern governments, there also are pressures in the North against efforts to challenge public policies by governments and constituencies that view these activities as "political" and therefore inappropriate.

In theory and sometimes in practice, those organizations least dependent on government resources are the most free to advocate changed policies. However, some NGOs accepting funds from governments have found that their relationship, rather than inhibiting criticism, has given them access to and credibility with governmental decisionmakers. Some NGOs also have found that identification in the public mind through advocacy and education with a given crisis may actually strengthen their position with governments.

As in the realm of education, individual agencies, rather than launching their own advocacy efforts, may work through other organizations, corporate or individual. In early 1990, an international NGO delegation organized by the International Council of Voluntary Agencies visited El Salvador, following the offensive of November 1989 by the Frente Farabundo Martí para la Liberación Nacional (FMLN). Confronting the government harassment of NGOs and churches, the group expressed solidarity with NGO counterparts; it met with the Salvadoran president and senior government officials to urge a change in the regime's policies; and, upon returning, it pressed members of Congress and the executive branch to reform US policies.

There is tension between efforts to change government policies, whether in developing or developed countries, and the principle of nonpartisanship. The perceived perils of political activism have limited the programs by many humanitarian groups. In countries such as the United Kingdom, lobbying for political change by charitable organizations is prohibited.

At the same time, advocacy for humanitarian principles is viewed increasingly as an appropriate activity for organizations engaged in the relief of suffering. This includes working to ensure adequate humanitarian space and addressing the ways in which government policies are implicated in such suffering.

Given the variety of views in this area, it is difficult to establish communitywide guidelines. In general, organizations that consider the conduct or support of advocacy as central to their raison d'être should review the extent to which these activities are compatible with enacting programs in conflicts. Conversely, agencies that eschew these activities should decide whether they are fulfilling their responsibility if they are not directly or indirectly trying to change harmful policies because armed conflict is the cause of the distress they seek to address.

Agency Culture

The seventh benchmark for institutional decisionmaking about humanitarian action can be termed "agency culture." The concept includes an organization's way of approaching its tasks, its relationships with other agencies, its self-image and public image, and its standard operating procedures. Activities in armed conflicts need to be compatible with a given institution's culture and also should fit into a particular historical and cultural context.

Providing assistance and protection in armed conflicts is a task of great delicacy. The kind of interactions between aid personnel and political authorities that are routine in development programs become highly charged when war rages. One rule of thumb frequently cited by practitioners is that if a given aid organization is criticized equally by the warring parties, it is probably proceeding well. The objective is not an absence but a balanced dose of controversy.

As indicated earlier, each belligerent can be expected to seek to use the humanitarian aid provided, as well as its providers, for its own purposes. Protagonists also may be expected to try to cast doubt upon the integrity of humanitarian efforts in the territory claimed by their adversaries. In short, agencies must be prepared for controversy.

The Salvadoran and Guatemalan governments often criticized international aid organizations during the 1980s for supporting their respective insurgencies. For their part, insurgents argued that efforts to assist people in government-held areas were helping to entrench unjust policies and to prolong warfare. The various charges contributed to the conflicts and made it more difficult for assistance to reach people in need. The question "What is your agency doing to relieve immediate suffering?" gave way to the question "Whose side are you on?"

The cultures of some agencies equip them better than others for navigating such troubled waters. Among UN agencies, UNICEF is generally perceived as functioning in civil wars without conferring recognition to insurgent political and military forces. Its history of involvement with women and children in such conflicts began in the late 1940s in China. UNICEF is also experienced at generating media attention, mobilizing resources, and responding quickly and flexibly. Thus it was the obvious choice (although not a perfect match) for the lead agency role in OLS.

The World Food Programme generally has not been viewed this way, despite its one-billion-dollar annual delivery of food aid, much of it in war zones. In recent years, changes in the WFP's institutional culture and the perception of its donors and recipients have enabled the organization to play a larger role in conflicts. UNHCR's mandate involves challenging governments where need be to protect the interests of refugees, a task it has assumed with greater vigor in recent years.

If one sine qua non for involvement in conflicts is an ability to deal with controversy, another is a tolerance of ambiguity. In 1984–1985 as groups in Great Britain and the United States sought to mobilize assistance for starving people in Ethiopia, some NGOs downplayed the complicity of the Mengistu government's resettlement policies in creating hunger. These were "political" matters outside the purview of "humanitarian" agencies.

Agencies were somewhat more forthright in presenting the Khmer Rouge's role in creating widespread famine among Cambodians, or Idi Amin's massive human rights abuses in Uganda. Confronting such questions about the nature of regimes may seem a diversion in the face of imminent starvation. However, as indicated in the discussion of contextualization, aid agencies ignore these questions at their peril.

As an agency contemplates involvement in a particular conflict, matters of institutional culture become critical. What is the agency's comfort level in dealing with controversy? Is it willing to operate in circumstances where normal written agreements with host political authorities are not possible? Is it prepared to wrestle with complex questions of international law and national sovereignty in order to win and maintain humanitarian access? Is it willing to take a close look at the links between providing aid and sustaining questionable policies and practices? Is it prepared to make and stand behind difficult choices in no-win situations?

There should be a compatible "fit" between a given agency, its constituency, and the tasks it undertakes. In tackling humanitarian challenges

In many countries in Latin America, the space for humanitarian action by churches, human rights and other voluntary agencies continues to be violated by parties to armed conflicts. Once again in 1991, we have witnessed brutal killings of humanitarian workers for the sole reason that they have tried to help the victims of massive human rights violations. The right to life, to food and to protection is embodied in international humanitarian law, and humanitarian efforts should be respected by all.
International Council of Voluntary Agencies, 1992[9]

in complex emergencies, if an agency fails to carry its constituency with it, its programs and resources will suffer.

Having assessed the terrain and taken agency culture into account, some organizations may proceed with humanitarian activities. Others may be well advised to forgo involvement in certain armed conflicts, or perhaps in complex emergencies altogether.

OPERATIONAL STRATEGIES

After examining the core functions in relieving life-threatening suffering, and after determining which organizations are able to perform certain functions best, agencies are well positioned to decide whether or not to act, and, if so, along what lines.

Continuing the progression from the general to the specific, the following section identifies institutional issues needing more attention as a given agency takes action. The issues include the particular relief inputs to be provided; appropriate personnel policies and procedures; coordination within a given agency and with other agencies; media relations; matters of cost; and local relationships.

In contrast to the subjects treated above, the terrain here has been more thoroughly mapped. Many agencies already have their own handbooks that address particular operational issues; the following section is accordingly briefer. For the convenience of agencies that want more details, a sampling of existing materials is included in the Selected Bibliography. Once again, although the issues identified in this section are generic, the specific operational challenges presented by armed conflicts are highlighted.

Emergency Relief Inputs

Considerable attention has been directed recently to the ingredients of emergency assistance. Regarding items such as food and medicine, attention has been devoted to the scale of the resources and their appropriateness. There are many examples of communities being inundated by inappropriate food, outdated medicines, and clothes for the wrong climate. A particularly vivid case concerns the donation of U.S. Army clothing for use inside Afghanistan, a shipment that was later redirected to a non-conflict setting in which the United States was not involved militarily. In these circumstances, communities are faced with recovering both from the initial disaster and from the international response to that disaster.

A growing number of agencies now try, whenever possible and with varying degrees of success, to purchase and transport resources from locations close to their final destination—ideally from within the affected country itself or, next best, from neighboring country suppliers. Benefits often accrue in cost savings as well as appropriateness. For instance, in addition to channeling food aid from Europe and North America, NGOs, using funds from private sources and the U.S. government, responded to serious shortages in war-wracked Tigray with food purchased in Tigray itself, using local currency, transport, and management.

International aid programs in general, and responses to armed conflicts in particular, have been heavily criticized for providing resources that donors are prepared to give, rather than those that are most needed. Although some relief items may be formally exempted from "tied aid" requirements, many agencies are under pressure to "buy American" or "buy Japanese," and to use whatever their constituencies would like to provide.

Greater attention also is being paid to the effects, positive and negative, of food and other relief supplies on local producers and suppliers. In Somalia, where pilfered international food aid became a staple in an otherwise languishing economy, relief organizations sought to limit this abuse by distributing food for direct consumption within feeding centers rather than providing food to be taken home. Efforts also were made to flood the economy with food, to reduce its value to unscrupulous hoarders, and to make it more widely available and affordable.

The targeting and duration of relief activities also are receiving more critical review, particularly in civil wars where international food aid may fuel the conflicts and create ongoing dependence on outside assistance. Agencies are now acknowledging the likelihood that food aid will be subject to abuse in chronically food-deficit countries in which military governments are challenged by armed insurgencies. Thus new CRS guidelines do not insist that all leakage be prevented or that relief supplies not prolong a conflict. Instead, a more modest and realistic test is imposed: Relief supplies should not fuel a conflict or add to the existing jeopardy of civilian populations.

Personnel, Policies, and Procedures

Recent experience suggests that the personnel policies and procedures of many humanitarian organizations are ill-suited to the circumstances of armed conflicts. "Standard operating procedures" do not necessarily

In the context of a conflict [in Bosnia-Herzegovina] which has as its very objective the displacement of people, we find ourselves confronted with a major dilemma. To what extent do we persuade people to remain where they are, when that choice could well jeopardize their lives and liberties? On the other hand, if we help them to move do we not become an accomplice to "ethnic cleansing"? Although our presence has not prevented "ethnic cleansing" as such, I do believe that international presence has made and will make a difference. In the absence of adequate legal principles or any mechanism for enforcing their compliance, new approaches should be explored to ensure effective international presence that bring together peace-keeping forces, humanitarian relief agencies and human rights observers.
Sadoka Ogata,
UN High Commissioner
for Refugees, 1993[10]

include provisions that are essential to function in nonstandard situations. Existing procedures are often too restrictive or altogether silent on critical points.

A host of security-related precautions are crucial to the safety of staff and the viability of activities. These include ground rules regarding commitment of staff to, and their evacuation from, insecure situations; communications procedures for use within a given country and to reach regional and international headquarters; and prominent identification of agency staff, vehicles, and relief supplies by recognizable logos. Faced with such matters, agencies whose main preoccupations are with development activities may be on uncertain ground in tackling emergencies in war zones, even in countries familiar to them.

Moreover, the selection and training of personnel for posting in settings of armed conflict require far greater attention than they have received in the past. The earlier finding that in the Sudan during 1989 the professionalism of aid institutions and officials left much to be desired appears to be equally applicable to humanitarian activities during the 1980s in Central America and 1990s in the Persian Gulf.

A lack of qualified people was apparent in 1990–1991, when simultaneous major emergencies in Somalia, Liberia, and Iraq exhausted the reservoir of trained personnel available to many UN organizations, governments, and NGOs. Subsequent arrangements between the Norwegian and Danish Refugee Councils and UN organizations to provide skilled persons quickly have capitalized on lessons learned then.

Given the risk and hardship involved in conflicts, many humanitarian agencies have relied on junior rather than more seasoned staff. NGOs and the United Nations alike have been criticized for excessive use in recent African emergencies of inexperienced Western staff instead of reliance on African expertise closer at hand. In the Persian Gulf crisis, expatriate medical personnel flown in from abroad drew salaries ten times greater than those of Jordanian doctors, many of whom were then unemployed. Educated Iraqis sought jobs as drivers for aid programs while inexperienced expatriates were brought in to run major operations.

Aid officials concede privately that conflicts often are viewed as a training ground for neophytes rather than as challenges requiring battle-scarred veterans. One suggested improvement involves field deployment of junior staff as understudies to more senior officials. The formation within the UN Volunteers of a special section for emergency relief is a step in the right direction.

In light of the special demands posed by conflicts, new attention is being directed to changes in personnel procedures governing deployment, rotation, evacuation, remuneration, and career progression. Following the much-publicized shortage of UN personnel in Somalia during a critical period of deepening famine in 1991–1992, the United Nations is also reviewing ground rules for deploying, evacuating, insuring, and paying its emergency staff. Consideration is being given to allowing UN officials with disaster mandates to be subject to guidelines different from those binding other international civil servants. In reviewing these procedures, the United Nations is comparing notes with the ICRC, which has managed to sustain its presence virtually uninterrupted throughout conflicts in Somalia and elsewhere, though not without significant loss of life.

Training might address another recurring problem among practitioners in wartime. While shared peril might be expected to foster greater collegiality across agency lines, many staff remain preoccupied with their own programs and take little interest in the work of others. In the Sudan, NGOs already carrying out programs and in a good position to help assess needs and plan activities were not consulted by the United Nations when it launched OLS, which nevertheless counted on their cooperation. History repeated itself in Somalia, where NGO expertise was enlisted only belatedly by UN officials.

Lack of collegiality is not unique to UN officials, however. For their part, some NGOs in the Sudan were outspoken in their criticism of OLS, despite its success in expanding their own humanitarian space. At the same time, several exhibited surprising lack of judgment, political naïveté, disregard of religious sensitivities, and lack of a broader policy orientation. There was also a reluctance among some NGOs receiving UN resources to comply with standard reporting requirements. Similar criticisms have been raised of private groups working among Afghan refugees along the Pakistan border and with Cambodians in Thailand.

Agencies now are realizing that operations in war zones require more specialized training than is needed even for many natural disasters. Special requirements may include awareness of gender aspects of assistance and protection, familiarity with international law, and sensitivity to issues of conflict resolution. With such special needs in mind, the Disaster Management Training Program of DHA/UNDRO and UNDP has developed materials on Displaced Persons in Civil Conflicts and International Law, Disasters, and Armed Conflict. Many other agencies are actively reviewing their personnel policies and revising and expanding their training programs.

It is worthwhile for agencies to consider the development of a cadre of experienced staff for rapid deployment, and a career development system that makes deployment feasible in human terms. A proposal resulting from an internal UN evaluation of field operations is circulating to create an elite corps of UN emergency specialists, a new kind of fire brigade to be called Fonctionnaires Sans Frontières. Also useful would be the availability of more training in applicable international law and in the political, economic, religious, and cultural contexts surrounding emergencies.

Coordination

The experience of mounting and maintaining humanitarian operations in wartime suggests that coordination problems, sizable in most natural disasters and development activities, are still more complicated in armed conflicts. Although aid practitioners favor coordination, and donors insist on it, few agencies wish to be coordinated. Many are reluctant to pay the costs that effective coordination requires.

Once again, the Sudan experience is illustrative. During the period from March to September 1989, officials in New York directed separate operations carried out from Khartoum in government-controlled areas of the south and from Nairobi in insurgent-controlled areas. The principle of nonpartisanship was served by managing overall coordination from neither of the warring camps. Although they were balanced and perceived as even-handed by both sides, the arrangements created other problems. WFP representatives in both Khartoum and Nairobi took their orders from WFP headquarters in Rome but reported on their activities to the OLS in New York.

Since October 1989, the focal point of coordination has been in Khartoum, to which the Nairobi-based "southern sector" operations reported. The new arrangements have not worked as well, with the insurgents charging that OLS has become more susceptible to Sudan government pressure and less evenhanded. The new arrangements also have made reporting difficult for UNICEF workers in Nairobi, who have continued to report to UNICEF headquarters in New York as well as to the OLS headquarters in Khartoum.

History has repeated itself in other UN decisions. Humanitarian activities in Angola are coordinated from Luanda, including operations in UNITA-controlled areas. Operations in Somalia are coordinated from territory in southern Mogadishu controlled by a single powerful faction. In each instance, the appearance of partiality has undermined relief operations. Available alternatives include managing relations with the host authorities in the capital city while setting up parallel contacts with opposition forces outside the country. In short, while coordination arrangements that appear to make administrative sense may be fraught with negative political implications, more evenhanded arrangements may make coordination more difficult.

*T*oday the UN has recognized the right to humanitarian assistance. . . . Once the right to intervene on humanitarian grounds is established, we shall have to develop and implement a right to intervention on democratic grounds to guarantee that human rights are respected everywhere.
Michel Rocard, former prime minister of France, 1991[11]

After the initial blitz of activities by the Allied Coalition, the United Nations played the central role in coordinating the international humanitarian response after the Gulf War. As indicated earlier, association with UN economic sanctions and military actions was a political liability in some quarters for UN agencies, humanitarian organizations, and some other non-UN groups, too. Moreover, the growing involvement of the Security Council in humanitarian crises elevates them to a new level of visibility and action. At the same time, it injects these crisis with a higher political content and may reduce the ability of the United Nations to coordinate humanitarian activities accordingly.

NGOs and the ICRC face similar difficulties to the extent that they operate programs on both or all sides of conflicts. They, too, require additional staff and additional coordination within their own ranks. Because of the importance of evenhandedness, they are often reluctant to allow themselves to be coordinated, particularly when such coordination, mediated by the United Nations or host authorities, restricts their operating space. While they are willing to accept additional resources generated by UN appeals, many NGOs are reluctant to pay the price of collaborative programming and reporting. This has reinforced the perception that some NGOs are "loose cannons," long on good intentions and energy but lacking in discipline and expertise.

In fact, coordination is somewhat foreign to NGO culture, whose self-image is to be flexible, innovative, and unbureaucratic. NGOs are reluctant to commit themselves to the kind of regular consultations that are routine in the corporate, governmental, and intergovernmental worlds. They opt to do rather than to talk about doing. Yet the coordination committees that they set up in northern Iraq and Cambodia greatly increased their effectiveness, and many are prepared to cooperate, if not to be coordinated.

In remarks during the General Assembly debates in late 1991 on strengthening UN coordination of humanitarian activities, the ICRC welcomed the creation of a high-level coordinator in New York and pledged to share information fully. In the interest of preserving its independence, however, the ICRC made it clear that it would not allow its activities to be coordinated by DHA.

Donor governments, while demanding the coordinated use of the resources they provide, often proceed in ways that make coordination more difficult. They usually select the channels for their resources—UNICEF or WFP, the ICRC, or NGOs, for example—that best accomplish their objectives. In several conflicts, this has created problems for whoever was in charge. A donor earmarking funds for specific activities and communities also has made coordination more difficult.

In short, as aid practitioners move to set up humanitarian activities, they need to give careful thought to the nature, structures, and costs of coordination. Policymakers and policy managers in all humanitarian institutions should clarify their expectations for coordination and its relative priority in the commitment of agency time and resources.

Media Relations

Humanitarian practitioners responding to life-threatening emergencies deal regularly with the media. They receive numerous requests for information about the nature of the crisis; how work is proceeding and how much it costs; how a given agency performs; and how the host government or the insurgents behave.

Answering such questions is sometimes difficult because up-to-date information is not available from overseas staff. Normal reporting, in which field personnel give to headquarters monthly information about development activities, project expenditures, and personnel matters, is not adequate in faster-paced, war-related emergencies.

In Iraq in early 1991, the appearance virtually overnight of some 1.6 million displaced Kurds on the Turkish border overloaded information systems, to say nothing of the capacity of the aid agencies. As with the flight six months earlier of some 850,000 third-country nationals and 300,000 Palestinians from Kuwait and Iraq, UN phones were ringing off the hook in Geneva and New York as well as in the region of the Turkish border. Yet officials were hard-pressed to provide the necessary data.

Beyond the problems of maintaining up-to-date and comprehensive information, forthright answers to legitimate inquiries sometimes are avoided because they would put pressure on relationships with donor or host governments, insurgents, or others whose ongoing collaboration and trust agencies need. Candor may also undercut sensitive negotiations to enlist the cooperation of the authorities or to gain access to vulnerable populations.

What were the views of the UN High Commissioner for Refugees—the media asked—on the unwillingness of the Turkish government to open its border to Iraqi refugees, or of the coalition's reluctance to insist that it do so? How did the organization view the interdiction of boat people seeking refuge in the United States from a Haiti wracked by a military coup and the effects of an economic embargo? What were the High Commissioner's views on the swift German recognition of breakaway Croatia? In some instances, UNHCR made public comments; in others, it chose not to do so.

High-visibility declarations—even on issues clearly within an agency's mandate and competence—may create problems with contributors or constituents, who sometimes are less willing to support humanitarian activities geared to help victims of conflicts than of "natural" disasters. Some NGOs seeking funds for Ethiopians facing starvation in 1984 avoided telling the media and their constituencies the extent to which the Ethiopian government was responsible for the 1984 famine. The same government soon frustrated relief activities. When NGOs contributed Ethiopian relief to reconstruction and development activities, they faced media and public criticism for betraying the wishes of donors.

*W*hile the principle of noninterference in the internal affairs of a sovereign power has long been a tenet of international law, the television images of these pathetic children swept it aside, and allied forces eventually were forced by public pressure to go into Iraq to protect the Kurds and feed the hungry.
Walter B. Wriston, former CEO of the Chrysler Corporation, 1992[12]

The media also can be an important ally. Media exposure of human need has frequently generated contributions to private agencies and pressure on donor governments to respond. Many aid organizations also attach great importance to having their own activities publicized. Those committed to education and advocacy, as noted earlier, have their own reasons for enlisting coverage. Cultivation of the media thus becomes a major activity.

Media relations carried out by UN agencies, donor governments, and Northern NGOs sometimes raise problems for those in need of assistance. After the 1984–1985 famine, Ethiopian representatives of an NGO consortium made a follow-up tour to North America. Congressional staffers who met with them in Washington expected, and received, thanks for working on quick passage of legislation that provided prompt assistance. They were taken aback, however, by criticism that the media portrayal of the famine and its victims, and congressional action based on it, had been insulting and humiliating.

If, as noted above, organizational culture is a key ingredient in deciding whether to engage in, continue in, or withdraw from a given disaster, the requirements of media relations should be reflected upon more seriously. While allies in generating awareness of a crisis, the media also can be counted on to ask tough questions, expect clear answers, and demand rigorous accountability. Agencies that cannot stand intense heat would be well advised to stay out of this kitchen.

Cost-Related Issues

Responding to emergencies in war is more expensive than in most other disasters. The earlier discussion of accountability noted various ways in which civil wars raise the costs of operations. A realistic assessment of such costs should figure prominently in agency decisionmaking. Considerations of cost-effectiveness are also relevant.

As already noted, the Sudan study was unable to determine the exact cost of OLS aid. Reliable and comparable data on the operations of various agencies, UN and otherwise, were simply unavailable. Comparisons between costs of operations in the Sudan and in other armed conflicts, while beyond the scope of the study, would have proved virtually impossible. Judgments of cost-effectiveness were even more problematic.

Experience suggests that in their desire to get into the action, many organizations underestimate the costs of wartime operations. Planning under duress and seeking to appear quick off the mark, they undercount the costs of staff deployment and rotation, communications and logistic support, and monitoring and evaluation. The duration of agency involvement is also frequently underestimated. Supposedly short-term interventions often require a longer presence. Although many humanitarian organizations are hardly international ambulance chasers, they often lack the organizational safeguards to assure that decisions be made with foreseeable costs and unforeseeable contingencies in mind.

Recent experience makes it worthwhile to repeat the Sudan case study's recommendation that agencies exercise greater restraint in getting involved in complex emergencies. Many organizations believe they have a contribution to make, but some underestimate the time and resources needed. Those that proceed should be guided by more realistic cost calculations.

The costs for other activities should also be considered. Is a given agency prepared to make the kind of investment on a per-beneficiary basis that effective relief—particularly of wartime suffering—requires? UNICEF estimates that it must spend twenty dollars on emergency programs (in natural disasters and civil wars combined) to produce the impact of a single dollar spent elsewhere. Agencies should do a careful assessment of the costs and benefits of their overall activities, particularly their development objectives, that arise from involvement in a particular emergency.

Local Relationships

Much of the preceding discussion has concentrated on the positions of major international actors. However, each of the issues reviewed also has a special meaning for indigenous participants in humanitarian activities, be they hosting political or military authorities or nongovernmental agencies. In fact, relationships with local institutions should interest international actors, considering the difficulties of establishing and managing programs effectively without their assistance.

Concerning personnel, for example, most international agencies must rely on a country's nationals to implement humanitarian activities. In fact, "local hires" may constitute the majority of project staff. In 1992 the ICRC's office in Nairobi had about 130 expatriates connected to it, many of them detailed to Somalia, the Sudan, Ethiopia, and Eritrea. At the same time, there were 600 local staff based in Kenya alone, including administrative and logistic support personnel. Operations by the United Nations, donor governments, and particularly NGOs may draw even more heavily on local staff.

The most dangerous tasks in wartime often fall to nationals. They tend to be the ones on the front lines—indeed frequently crossing them—while international staff remain in capital cities (which can also be unsafe). Although expatriate medical personnel have been killed in Somalia and the Sudan, the highest casualty rate has been among local truck drivers. Throughout the Horn of Africa, relief vehicles have drawn fire and detonated land mines, with great loss of life and limb. Of the eleven humanitarian personnel who lost their lives in the Sudan in 1992, most were Sudanese in the employment of either the U.S. government or the EC.

In earlier discussions of mutuality and appropriateness, the desirability of enlisting local personnel was noted. Yet there are certain risks and drawbacks. Since humanitarian activities in armed conflicts often are controversial, local people who assume leadership roles may increase their own vulnerability. Serving as the local eyes and ears for the world community, they and their families frequently are viewed as international agents.

Thus Sri Lankans are likely to be more vulnerable to pressures from their government and from the Tamil Tigers of Eelam than are international personnel. They also lack the relative protection that an outsider's status and a foreign passport may confer. Guatemalan employees of international organizations orchestrating the return of refugees in early 1993 were subject to pressures from the same regime that produced the refugees in the first place.

A myriad of personnel questions results. Does an international humanitarian organization bear a responsibility for the risks that indigenous organizations and individuals run? Should security and evacuation ground rules for foreign nationals also apply to local staffs? Should the personnel policies of local partner organizations with which an international agency works be of interest and concern?

Media relations also affect local relationships. Many of the questions asked about humanitarian activities, for example, are raised by the representatives of radio, television, and print media on the scene of various

*T*he urgency of peace in Africa is hard to overstate. Many of the recent famines in sub-Saharan countries have been directly connected with military conflicts (for example, in Ethiopia, Sudan, Somalia, Uganda, Chad, Nigeria and Mozambique). Wars not only lead to massacres and associated horrors, they also destroy crops and other economic resources, undermine traditional patterns of livelihood, discourage economic investments and capital formation and also disrupt the normal operations of trade and commerce. They also help consolidate the grip of the military on civil life and tend to disrupt civil liberties, including the freedom of the press, which is an important safeguard against famines and other man-made catastrophes.
Amartya Sen, Harvard University, 1990[13]

crises. Answers are expected from humanitarian officials on the spot. To what extent will indigenous staff be permitted, or encouraged, to make themselves available to the media? What kind of training about the organization's policies and activities is desirable?

In the case of the Joint Relief Partnership (an undertaking by Ethiopia's national Catholic, Orthodox, and Lutheran churches, with international support from CRS, LWF, and donor governments), the involvement of outside religious groups was a matter of some sensitivity. Publicizing international connections would have created problems with the host government, which insisted that the effort be entirely local. Yet ignoring the roles of outsiders might not have satisfied international needs. Media issues are of such importance and sensitivity that clear policy guidelines and training are needed.

In sum, because armed conflicts make local institutions and personnel the altogether critical link between the international humanitarian system and those in need, issues related to capacity and exposure of those local links require attention.

NOTES

1. Independent Commission on International Humanitarian Issues, *Winning the Human Race?* (London: Zed Books, 1988): 71–72.
2. Catholic Relief Services, *Guidelines on Humanitarian Assistance in Conflict Situations* (Baltimore, Md.: CRS, 1992): 6.
3. Larry Minear, *Helping People in the Age of Conflict: Toward a New Professionalism in U.S. Voluntary Humanitarian Assistance* (New York and Washington, D.C.: Inter-Action, 1988): 40.
4. National Public Radio's *Morning Edition,* January 14, 1993.
5. Refugee Policy Group, *Internally Displaced Persons in Africa: Assistance Challenges and Opportunities* (Washington, D.C.: Refugee Policy Group, 1992): 1–2 of original draft.
6. Larry Minear, *Humanitarianism Under Siege: A Critical Review of Operation Lifeline Sudan* (Trenton, N.J.: Red Sea Press, 1991): 112.
7. Minear, *Helping People*: 70.

8. International Council of Voluntary Agencies and UNHCR, "Criteria for Building NGO/UNHCR Partnerships," 1992: 3.

9. International Council of Voluntary Agencies, "Statement to the 48th Session of the UN Commission on Human Rights," February 1992: 2.

10. Sadako Ogata, "Refugees and World Peace." Symposium on Strengthening the United Nations—Peace and Environment, Tokyo, January 1993: 15.

11. Michel Rocard, *Europe and the United States,* Critical Issues, no. 2 (New York: Council on Foreign Relations, April 1992): 35.

12. Walter B. Wriston, *The Twilight of Sovereignty: How the Information Revolution Is Transforming Our World* (New York: Charles Scribner's Sons, 1992): 138–139.

13. Amartya Sen, *Public Action to Remedy Hunger* (New York: The Hunger Project, 1990): 24.

Evolving Humanitarian Standards: Toward a Code of Conduct for Armed Conflicts

Chapter One identified guiding principles to provide a framework for humanitarian assistance and protection. Chapter Two enumerated emerging policy guidelines for more effective humanitarian action. Chapter Three considers how these principles and policy guidelines may form the basis for a code of conduct for humanitarian practitioners operating in war zones.

It was earlier acknowledged that organizations and officials engaged in humanitarian assistance and protection work differ among themselves as to the scope, feasibility, opportunity costs, and utility of a code of conduct. "Why do we need a code of conduct?" some ask. After all, the range of viewpoints on issues of principle and practice that caused the failure of previous efforts to develop a code still exist, and reduce the chances of forging agreement in the future. Moreover, the issues themselves are so sensitive and public trust so fragile that the effort necessary to achieve consensus could be counterproductive. Why not simply proceed, without high-sounding rhetoric, to find practical areas where meaningful cooperation and better programming is possible?

Others disagree, asking rhetorically, "How can the performance of humanitarian organizations be improved *without* a code of conduct?" A code is urgently needed because functioning effectively in armed conflicts is so complex; the exposure of civilian populations is so perilous; and the stakes for the international community are so high. In fact, unless humanitarian organizations take steps on their own, more rigorous accountability will be imposed on them. The decibel level of criticism surrounding the UN and NGO paralysis in Somalia in 1991–1992 and the failure to avoid deaths due to starvation and exposure in Bosnia during the winter of 1992–1993 suggest that faith in the humanitarian enterprise may be wearing thin.

Those who highlight the heterogeneity of views and the difficulties of finding common ground have a point. But recent experience makes highly diverse agencies somewhat more willing to struggle with these issues. The time is ripe for the humanitarian community as a whole to affirm certain broad principles, and for individual agencies and groups of agencies to articulate and implement standards for themselves. In addition to discussions at the international level, consultation among like-minded groups by region or subregion also might advance agreement about elements of a code. This handbook, including this final chapter on issues related to a code, is intended to contribute to progress in this area.

PRINCIPLES

The eight Providence Principles articulated in Chapter One provide a skeleton for a future code of conduct. Stated in their current form and refined over time, they may receive wide endorsement by major humanitarian actors, both international and indigenous.

While it would be wrong to claim that there are no longer arguments regarding principles, disagreement emerges less at the level of definition than of implementation. While all the major actors agree that sovereignty should stand under the judgment of humanitarian norms, vast differences among them remain about when and how violations of humane standards in the name of sovereignty should be challenged and overridden.

Moreover, broad agreement on individual principles may mask the differentiating relative priority attached to each principle. Strict adherence to the principles of *independence* and *accountability* may reduce or curtail activities directed toward *the relief of life-threatening suffering*. Quick action in life-threatening emergencies may not allow the full use of local institutions, which considerations *appropriateness* would dictate. Faithfulness to the principle of *proportionality* may be tested by situations in which insistence on *accountability* deprives people of a fair share of aid resources.

A recurrent theme of this handbook is that individual principles are not absolute, existing in solitary splendor. Rather, each principle exists in dynamic tension with other and sometimes competing principles. The fact that individual organizations need to make their own determinations about relative priorities does not mean that a code of conduct is less desirable or attainable.

TASKS OF THE HUMANITARIAN COMMUNITY

A key task of the community of humanitarian organizations as a whole, beyond providing assistance and protection to those in need, is to affirm stated principles as goals toward which it will strive. Sharing basic objectives,

F ar-reaching changes internationally and within the United Nations are essential if the world wishes to minimize the suffering of populations trapped by civil-war induced starvation. Member states need to decide whether, and then how, the United Nations should be equipped to provide humanitarian relief in situations of large-scale violence.
Jan Eliasson,
UN Under-Secretary-General for Humanitarian Affairs, 1993[1]

humanitarian organizations face common challenges in carrying out their programs. The greater the sense of solidarity within the community as a whole, the greater the critical mass and momentum in carrying out its formidable tasks.

A common sense of purpose has very tangible payoffs. In dealing with governments or insurgent forces, a "common front" makes it more difficult to play some agencies off against others. Faced in October 1992 with a deterioration in security and with the sobering reality that an estimated 90 percent of relief supplies were failing to reach people in need, the UN Secretary-General's Special Representative for Somalia, Ambassador Mohammed Sahnoun, floated the possibility of a moratorium on humanitarian operations. With donor governments reluctant to withhold assistance and key aid agencies unwilling to cooperate,

the proposal was not pursued, although the idea was a creative one.

In theory, the necessary humanitarian space is more attainable when the humanitarian community negotiates a common agreement with authorities rather than when individual agencies make separate arrangements. Moreover, public confidence in the enterprise as a whole is undermined when humanitarian activities appear autarchic and when unscrupulous agencies appear to play by their own rules. A comprehensive mobilization of the international public makes more sense than a series of individual appeals.

However great the value of communitywide efforts, the diversity of principles, operating styles, and institutional cultures among the major actors makes joint action difficult. Even though bound by common values and even when confronted with common challenges, UN and government agencies, NGOs, and the ICRC nevertheless remain a bewilderingly pluralistic lot. Thrust together by the unifying force of a particular crisis, they soon allow centrifugal forces to take over.

Their diversity aggravates the difficulty of devising a single code for all practitioners. While it is hardly a fiction to speak of a single "humanitarian community," in reality a number of communities or perhaps subcommunities exist. A series of codes for different major sets of actors may be in order. In fact, to insist on a single code might result in a set of standards so innocuous that it can do little to improve operations.

Within each set of actors or subcommunities there is room for dialogue and common action. Recent experience suggests that the major sets of international and domestic actors have certain broad common approaches to humanitarian issues. Accordingly, it makes sense for each of the four pillars—UN agencies, governments, NGOs, and the Red Cross/Red Crescent movement—to work out its own code of conduct. Certainly, the process of hammering out a common approach within each of the four groupings itself represents a step in the direction of greater clarity and eventually perhaps of greater collegiality.

The various sets of actors are now at different points in the discussion process. In the UN family, DHA is beginning to give preliminary thought to the matter. Most donor governments have hardly begun the process among themselves. NGOs, perhaps the most diverse subcommunity, have tackled the challenge both at the international level and in individual countries, although common standards have thus far proved elusive. The Geneva-based Licross/Volags Steering Committee for Disasters is drafting a code of conduct in consultation with its member agencies. The Federation of Red Cross and Red Crescent Societies is developing a framework to guide members of the Red Cross in their relationships with military forces.

As the discussions move from the level of principles to that of operations, issues needing attention may also be better handled by the various subcommunities than by the humanitarian community as a whole. For example, there will be more common-held views among governments on the question of the appropriateness of using military forces in conducting aid activities than there will be among NGOs, although even among governments there are differences. Consensus on establishing a ceiling on administrative expenses may be more possible among NGOs than among UN agencies.

For all the common ground within subcommunities, there are significant differences within each of the sets of actors. The mandates, histories, and cultures of UNICEF and UNHCR, as well as recent changes in the terms of reference of the WFP, equip these organizations to deal with belligerents in civil wars better than other UN agencies. Nordic governments, which have a history of nonpartisan responses to human needs, are normally more welcome in highly politicized settings than is the United States. Some NGOs limit humanitarian work to countries in which they can count on their home government's blessing; others are less constrained.

As subcommunities pursue discussions with their own colleagues, they may discover greater common ground outside their own group than within. Some UN agencies frequently seem more like NGOs than like other members of the UN system. Some NGOs have

*W*e urge organizations involved in humanitarian activities to adopt codes of conduct for operating in conflict situations so as to better guarantee their neutrality and safety in delivering assistance and to increase their professionalism and accountability.
Refugee Policy Group, 1992[2]

more in common with governments than with other NGOs. Although such cross-linkages may make agreement on codes of conduct within a given subcommunity more difficult, they hardly make a communitywide code more feasible.

TASKS OF INDIVIDUAL AGENCIES

In the final analysis, humanitarian activities are carried out by individual organizations. Each agency struggles in individual and sometimes idiosyncratic ways with the issues raised by the principles and policy guidelines elaborated above. Each institution ultimately decides for itself what it does where, with whom, and for how long.

As indicated earlier, humanitarian agencies have their own mechanisms to ensure accountability. Individual NGOs are accountable to their own boards of directors. Bilateral donors consider themselves accountable to their parliaments, multilateral agencies to their member governments. Rather than seeking mechanisms to hold all actors to common standards, it therefore seems more feasible, and ultimately perhaps more effective, to encourage individual agencies and groups of agencies to set their own standards and police their own activities.

Consistency is not only more attainable but also more necessary within individual agencies than between or among them. It is accepted that different agencies will take diverse approaches to various armed conflicts. Applying principles to given situations will quite obviously involve judgment calls. However, it is important for the credibility of a given agency to apply, and to be seen as applying, consistent guidelines in charting its involvement across a wide range of conflicts.

For example, some international NGOs have decided to operate large programs in certain countries with very poor human rights records while not doing so in other countries with better records where the needs are just as great. "It is not always clear," points out an Oxfam-UK editorial, "how far such choices are purely historical and ad hoc, how much they are driven by donors, and how much they are determined by the political views of NGO staff. Why were so many more agencies operating with refugees in Thailand than inside Cambodia? Why were agencies willing to work under the controls imposed by the since-overthrown Ethiopia regime, but not those of a similar regime in Burma?"

An agency-by-agency approach may be more practical as well as more consistent. It reduces opportunity costs, staff time, and financial expenses required by a more inclusive approach. Tailoring the result to a given agency would also avoid differences between agencies that prefer to frame discussions of a code of conduct more broadly (for example, including

Rather than describing the ingredients of the humanitarian professional, we would serve ourselves better by talking about the competent, accountable, transparent, well-rounded generalist. He/she is the one with the wisdom to know when specialist skills are required and whence they can be mobilized. The seasoned generalist (the real professional) is the one who has the courage to deliberately "mix" peace-politics with humanitarian aid. He/she is the one who understands that any placement of humanitarian aid is by itself a political act. The only question concerns which kind of politics—whether in support of peace processes or in support of continuing conflict.
Harold Miller, Mennonite Central Committee, 1992[3]

reconstruction and development needs) and agencies that see themselves purely as managers of emergency programs.

Some agencies are making encouraging progress in their efforts to set standards for their own performance in conflicts. Over the years the ICRC has developed, put into practice, and refined perhaps the most clear and well-elaborated set of standards for its organization and staff. CRS in 1992 approved as agency-wide policy the guidelines referred to earlier. Oxfam-UK over the years has carried a sustained dialogue on these issues. The handbook is intended to stimulate still other organizations to pursue these issues and to learn from each other.

CODE ENFORCEMENT

The code of conduct outlined above represents common humanitarian principles accepted by organizations struggling collectively and working individually in the turbulent world of armed conflict. Such a code should not be viewed as legally binding or enforceable, but rather as a set of norms toward which humanitarian organizations strive.[]

While a code would stop short of being regulatory in nature, it would be more than purely hortatory. Its credibility would depend on its ability to enhance the quality of assistance and protection. That ability would be a function of the seriousness with which practitioners and agencies approached their obligations and, in the case of governments, of the extent to which a code were consistent with international law.

A code could also serve as an instrument around which peer pressure could be mobilized. Currently, few mechanisms are available for isolating "pariah" organizations that embrace the political causes of belligerents, advance the strategic agendas of donor governments, subvert the dignity of needy populations, or abuse the trust of contributors. A code could provide a basis for calling into question this aberrant behavior. There is also a certain appeal to the idea of increasing transparency and self-evaluation, both in its own right and as a means for dealing with a vigilant media and well-informed public.

A code would not guarantee that humanitarian activities would be more professionally managed. Agencies would still have to make judgments: some of them wise and vindicated by events, others less wise and overtaken by events. Over time, however, agencies increasingly would be expected to explain deviations from an accepted code. The expectations would work as a check against the extremes mentioned earlier of pure pragmatism unguided by humanitarian principle, and fidelity to humanitarian principle uninformed by the exigencies of conflicts.

WORK IN PROGRESS AND ISSUES FOR FURTHER ANALYSIS

The evolution of the humanitarian regime proceeds in unpredictable ways. Just as the principles identified in Chapter One are clearer now than a decade ago, further refinements may be expected in the coming years. There may also be temporary setbacks.

A number of initiatives now under way may contribute to enhancing the professionalism of humanitarian practitioners and to developing codes of conduct. These activities should be sustained and accelerated:

- Several UN organizations are developing training materials that will help personnel function more effectively in armed conflicts. They should take advantage of training resources and materials that already exist and identify elements for possible incorporation into a common set of materials. UNHCR, for example, is developing guidelines for staff on voluntary repatriation in conflict situations that could be useful to other UN staff.
- The International Council of Voluntary Agencies (ICVA) and the Henry Dunant Institute of the Red Cross movement have been exploring the possibility of reviewing the experience of aid practitioners in specific armed conflicts. This initiative should be encouraged and should share its findings with a wider circle of interested parties.
- The Licross/Volags Steering Committee for Disasters should continue work on a code of conduct that addresses broad principles of humanitarian action. While its code would be self-regulatory for the signatory NGOs, it also might be used as a basis for negotiating reciprocity with the United Nations and donor governments. Participating agencies, in exchange for partnership in UN operations, might receive certain benefits (such as use of communications facilities or evacuation options) not available to nonparticipating NGOs.
- The Federation of Red Cross and Red Crescent Societies is developing guidelines concerning relationships between NGOs and

*W*hat is required
... is a new
breed of
humanitarian, a combi-
nation of the humanitar-
ian visionary and the
humanitarian mechanic.
Arthur E. Dewey,
Former Deputy UN
High Commissioner for
Refugees, 1990[4]

military forces in natural disasters and armed conflicts. These guidelines should be circulated to stimulate wider discussion, especially among those who normally dismiss military assets as contributing to problems rather than resolving them.

- InterAction has recently developed for the first time a set of standards for its 143 U.S. member NGOs that covers a wide range of governance, management, and program issues, including some of those detailed in this handbook.

- The UN Under-Secretary-General for Humanitarian Affairs should promote intensive interagency discussions on humanitarian issues and provide a forum for exchanges between international civil servants and practitioners from other subcommunities. The perceived dichotomy between humanitarian assistance and human rights protections should be reviewed. Linkages between humanitarian activities, conflict resolution, peace, and development should be more systematically explored.

- Professional associations of NGOs at the national, regional, and international levels should be encouraged to review the possibility of promoting a common code of conduct, or of designing their own.

- The Organization of Economic Cooperation and Development (OECD) should be encouraged to hold discussions within the Development Assistance Committee on these issues, as should other groupings like CIREFCA at the regional level.

- To generate greater accountability for activities in conflicts, the creation of an "Aid Watch" organization should be explored. Such an organization could draw on the experience of nongovernmental human rights groups and networks. Committed to helping agencies perform more effectively, it could work to assure that principles and policy guidelines such as those discussed in this handbook are taken seriously by humanitarian institutions.

- The Humanitarianism and War Project should serve as a resource for individual agencies and groups of agencies reviewing these issues, using this handbook as a resource.

NOTES

1. Under-Secretary-General Jan Eliasson, in U.N. Department of Public Information, "Enlarging the UN's Humanitarian Mandate," December 1992: 1.

2. Refugee Policy Group, "Humanitarian Action in the Post Cold War Era," Background Paper and Conference Summary. Washington, D.C.: Refugee Policy Group, 1991: 17.

3. Harold Miller, Mennonite Central Committee, in correspondence with the Humanitarianism and War Project dated July 23, 1992: 2.

4. Arthur E. Dewey, "Refugees and Peace: A Strategy for the 1990s," *Journal of Refugee Studies* 3: 1 (1990): 24.

Selected Bibliography

BOOKS AND ARTICLES

Aboum, Tabyiegen A., Eshetu Chole, Koste Manibe, Larry Minear, Abdul Mohammed, Jennefer Sebstad, and Thomas G. Weiss, *A Critical Review of Operation Lifeline Sudan: A Report to the Aid Agencies* (Washington, D.C.: Refugee Policy Group, 1990).

Africa Watch, *Evil Days: 30 Years of War and Famine in Ethiopia* (New York and Washington, D.C.: Human Rights Watch, 1991).

Ahlström, Christer, *Casualties of Conflict: Report for the World Campaign for the Protection of Victims of War* (Uppsala, Sweden: Department of Peace and Conflict Research, Uppsala University, 1991).

Anderson, Mary B., and Peter J. Woodrow, *Rising from the Ashes: Disaster Response Toward Development* (Boulder, Colo.: Westview, 1989).

Amnesty International, *Women in the Frontline: Human Rights Violations Against Women* (London: Amnesty International, 1991).

Bettati, Mario, and Bernard Kouchner, *Le devoir d'ingérence* (Paris: Denoël, 1987).

Carter, Ashton B., William J. Perry, and John D. Steinbruner, *A New Concept of Cooperative Security* (Washington, D.C.: Brookings Institution, 1992).

Cuny, Frederick, *Disasters and Development* (New York: Oxford University Press, 1984).

Cuny, Frederick, Barry N. Stein, and Pat Reed (eds.), *Repatriation During Conflict in Africa and Asia* (Dallas, Tex.: Center for the Study of Societies in Crisis, 1992).

Damrosch, Lori Fisler, and David J. Scheffer (eds.), *Law and Force in the New International Order* (Boulder, Colo.: Westview, 1991).

Deng, Francis M., and Larry Minear, *The Challenges of Famine Relief: Emergency Operations in the Sudan* (Washington, D.C.: Brookings Institution, 1992).

Donnelly, Jack, *Universal Human Rights in Theory and in Practice* (Ithaca, N.Y.: Cornell University, 1989).

———. "Human Rights in the New World Order," *World Policy Journal* ix: 2 (1992): 249–277.

Forsythe, David P., *The Internationalization of Human Rights* (Lexington, Mass.: Lexington Books, 1991).

———. *Humanitarian Politics* (Baltimore, Md.: John Hopkins University Press, 1977).

Goldman, Robert B., and A. Jeyaratran Wilson, *From Independence to Statehood* (London: Pinter, 1984).

Gordenker, Leon, *Refugees in International Politics* (London: Croom-Helm, 1987).

Gordenker, Leon, and Thomas G. Weiss (eds.), *Soldiers, Peacekeepers and Disasters* (London: Macmillan, 1992).

Halperin, Morton H., and David J. Scheffer, *Self-Determination in the New World Order* (Washington, D.C.: Carnegie Endowment for International Peace, 1992).

Henkin, Louis, *Right v. Might* (New York: Council on Foreign Relations, 1991).

Independent Commission on International Humanitarian Issues, *The Dynamics of Displacement* (London: Zed Books, 1987).

———. *Famine: A Man-Made Disaster?* (New York: Random House, 1985).

———. *Modern War: The Humanitarian Challenge* (London: Zed Books, 1986).

———. *Winning the Human Race?* (London: Zed Books, 1988).

International Committee of the Red Cross, The Geneva Conventions of August 12, 1949. (Geneva: ICRC, 1949).

———. Protocols additional to the Geneva Conventions of 12 August 1949. (Geneva: ICRC, 1977).

Jean, François (ed.), *Populations in Danger* (London: John Libbey & Company, 1992).

Kalshoven, Frits (ed.), *Assisting the Victims of Armed Conflict and Other Disasters* (Dordrecht, Netherlands; Boston; and London: Martinus Nijhoff Publishers, 1989).

Kent, Randolph, *Anatomy of Disaster Relief* (London: Pinter, 1987).

Lake, Anthony (ed.), *After the Wars: Reconstruction in Afghanistan, Indochina, Central America, Southern Africa, and the Horn of Africa* (Washington, D.C.: Overseas Development Council, 1990).

Larkin, Mary Ann, Frederick C. Cuny, and Barry N. Stein (eds.), *Repatriation Under Conflict in Central America* (Washington, D.C.: Center for Immigration and Refugee Assistance, 1991).

Lyons, Gene, and Michael Mostanduno, *Beyond Westphalia? National Sovereignty and International Intervention* (Berkeley: University of California Press, 1993).

Macalister-Smith, Peter, *International Humanitarian Assistance: Disaster Relief Actions in International Law and Organization* (Boston: Martinus Nijhoff, 1985).

MacFarlane, Neil S., and Thomas G. Weiss, "Regional Organizations and Regional Security," *Security Studies* 2: 3 (Fall/Winter 1992–1993): 6–37.

Middle East Watch, *Needless Deaths in the Gulf War* (New York and Washington, D.C.: Human Rights Watch, 1991).

Minear, Larry, *Helping People in an Age of Conflict: Toward a New Professionalism in U.S. Voluntary Humanitarian Assistance* (New York and Washington, D.C.: InterAction, 1988).

Minear, Larry, U.B.P. Chelliah, J. Crisp, J. Mackinlay, and T. G. Weiss, *United Nations Coordination of the International Humanitarian Response to the Gulf Crisis, 1990–92.* Occasional Paper #13. Providence, R.I.: Thomas J. Watson Jr. Institute, 1992.

Minear, Larry, et al., *Humanitarianism Under Siege: A Critical Review of Operation Lifeline Sudan* (Trenton, N.J.: Red Sea Press, 1991).

Minear, Larry, Thomas G. Weiss, and Kurt M. Campbell, *Humanitarianism and War: Learning the Lessons from Recent Armed Conflicts.* Occasional Paper #8. Providence, R.I.: Thomas J. Watson Jr. Institute, 1991.

Minear, Larry, and Thomas G. Weiss, "Groping and Coping in the Gulf Crisis: Discerning the Shape of a New Humanitarian Order," *World Policy Journal* IX: 4 (Fall/Winter 1992–1993): 755–788.

Nichols, Bruce, "Rubberband Humanitarianism," *Ethics & International Affairs* 1 (1987): 191–210.

Patrnogic, J., and B. Jakovljevic, *Protection of Human Beings in Disaster Situations: A Proposal for Guiding Principles* (San Remo: International Institute for Humanitarian Law, 1989).

Scheffer, David J., "Toward a Modern Doctrine of Humanitarian Intervention," *The University of Toledo Law Review* 23 (1992): 253–293.

Sen, Amartya, *Poverty and Famines* (New York: Oxford University Press, 1981).

UNESCO, *International Dimensions of Humanitarian Law* (Dordrecht, Netherlands: Martinus Nijhoff, 1988).

Urquhart, Brian, "The Role of the United Nations in the Iraq-Kuwait Conflict in 1990," *SIPRI Yearbook 1991: World Armaments and Disarmament* (Stockholm: SIPRI, 1991): 617–637.

Weiss, Thomas G., ed., *Collective Security in a Changing World* (Boulder, Colo.: Lynne Rienner, 1993).

Weiss, Thomas G., "New Challenges for UN Military Operations: Implementing an Agenda for Peace," *The Washington Quarterly* 16: 1 (Winter 1992): 51–66.

Weiss, Thomas G., and Jarat Chopra, "Sovereignty Is No Longer Sacrosanct: Codifying Humanitarian Intervention," *Ethics & International Affairs* 6 (1992): 95–117.

Weiss, Thomas G., and Larry Minear, *Humanitarianism Across Borders: Sustaining Civilians in Times of War* (Boulder, Colo.: Lynne Reinner, 1993).

White, Peter T., "A Little Humanity Amid the Horrors of War," *National Geographic* 170: 5 (November 1986).

TRAINING MATERIALS

Bureau for Refugee Programs, *Assessment Manual for Refugee Emergencies* (Washington, D.C.: U.S. Department of State, 1985).

Baccino-Astrada, Alma, *Manual on the Rights and Duties of Medical Personnel in Armed Conflicts* (Geneva: ICRC, 1982).

Cameron, M., and Y. Hofvander, *Manual of Feeding Infants and Young Children* (Rome: FAO, 1976).

Catholic Relief Services Guidelines for Humanitarian Assistance in Conflict Situations (Baltimore, Md.: CRS, 1992).

Cuny, Frederick, *Displaced Persons in Civil Conflict* (New York: UNDP Disaster Management Training Program, 1991).

———. *Displaced Persons in Civil Conflict: Trainers Guide* (New York: UNDP Disaster Management Training Program, 1991).

de Ville de Goyet, C., J. Seaman, and U. Geijer, *The Management of Nutritional Emergencies in Large Populations* (Geneva: WHO, 1978).

Emergency Manual: Man Made Disasters: Man's Violence Against Man and Nature (Rome: Caritas Internationalis, 1986, volume 2).

Field Directors' Handbook (London: Oxfam, 1980).

General Principles and Phasing of Response (Rome: World Food Programme, 1991).

A Guide to Food and Health Relief Operations for Disasters (New York: United Nations, 1977).

Helping Children in Difficult Circumstances, A Teacher's Manual (London: Save the Children Fund, 1991).

Implementation of International Humanitarian Law Protection of the Civilian Population and Persons Hors de Combat (Geneva: ICRC, 1991).

International Response to Emergencies (Geneva: International Council of Voluntary Agencies, August 1991).

Oxfam's Practical Guide to Selective Feeding Programmes (London: Oxford University Press, 1984).

Ressler, Everett M., Neil Boothby, and Daniel J. Steinbock, *Unaccompanied Children: Care and Protection in Wars, Natural Disasters and Refugee Movements* (London: Oxford University Press, 1988).

Simmonds, S., et al., *Refugee Community Health Care* (London: Oxford University Press, 1982).

Skeet, Muriel, *Manual for Disaster Relief Work* (London: Churchill Livingstone, 1977).
UNHCR, Coping with Stress in Crisis Situations (Geneva: UNHCR, 1992).
UNHCR Guidelines on the Protection of Refugee Women (Geneva: UNHCR, 1991).
UNHCR Guidelines on Refugee Children (Geneva: UNHCR, August 1988).
UNHCR Guidelines on Security (Geneva: UNHCR, July 1992).
UNHCR Handbook for Emergencies (Geneva: UNHCR, December 1982).
UNHCR Handbook for Social Services (Geneva: UNHCR, 1983).
UNHCR Trainer's Guide, Emergency Preparedness (Geneva: UNHCR, 1990).
UNHCR Training Module, Emergency Preparedness (Geneva: UNHCR, 1990).
Williamson, Jan, and Audrey Moser, *Unaccompanied Children in Emergencies: A Field Guide for Their Care and Protection* (International Social Service) (Norway: Redd Barna, UNHCR, and UNICEF, 1987).

THE HUMANITARIANISM AND WAR PROJECT: FORTHCOMING PUBLICATIONS

Minear, Larry, "Making the Humanitarian System Work Better," in Kevin Cahill (ed.), *A Framework for Survival: Health, Human Rights and Humanitarian Assistance in Conflicts and Disasters* (New York: Basic Books and Council on Foreign Relations, 1993).
Minear, Larry, and Thomas G. Weiss, *Humanitarianism and War: Reducing the Human Cost of Armed Conflict* (Boulder, Colo.: Lynne Rienner, 1994).
The United Nations Authority in Cambodia (Providence, R.I.: Thomas J. Watson Jr. Institute, 1993).
Weiss, Thomas G., and Jarat Chopra, "Sovereignty Under Siege: From Humanitarian Intervention to Humanitarian Space," in Gene Lyons and Michael Mastanduno, *Beyond Westphalia? National Sovereignty and International Intervention* (Berkeley: University of California Press, 1993).
Weiss, Thomas G., and Larry Minear, *Humanitarianism Across Borders: Sustaining Civilians in Times of War* (Boulder, Colo.: Lynne Rienner, 1993).

The Book and Authors

In Ethiopia and Angola, El Salvador and Nicaragua, Cambodia and Croatia, relief agencies have been concerned with the ravages of conflict, not only because of their disastrous impact on civilian populations, but also because of their threat to aid personnel, who have been harassed, held hostage, injured, and even killed. Aid convoys have been hijacked or detained, aid activities commandeered or shot down.

Responding to the complexities of today's challenges for humanitarian personnel, this handbook presents practical, illustrative, and creative approaches that practitioners can adopt in specific conflict arenas. The authors distill critical lessons from the recent experiences of aid professionals in UN agencies, the Red Cross and Red Crescent, governments, and private aid groups. They examine humanitarian principles, offer policy guidelines with checklists and benchmarks, propose operational strategies, and include a selected bibliography to help with further research. The handbook is based on the findings of the Humanitarianism and War Project, a three-year initiative conducted by Brown University's Watson Institute for International Studies and the Refugee Policy Group.

Larry Minear has worked on humanitarian and development issues since 1972 on behalf of Church World Service and Lutheran World Relief, two U.S. NGOs, and as a consultant to UN and U.S. government organizations. In 1972–1973, he managed a relief program in the southern Sudan. In 1990, he headed an international team that carried out a case study of Operation Lifeline Sudan. He has written extensively about humanitarian and development issues. He currently codirects, with Thomas G. Weiss, the Humanitarianism and War Project.

Thomas G. Weiss is associate director of the Thomas J. Watson Jr. Institute for International Studies and Associate Dean of the Faculty at Brown University. Previously he held a number of UN posts (at UNCTAD, the

UN Commission for Namibia, UNITAR, and ILO) and served as executive director of the International Peace Academy. He has written extensively about international organizations related to North-South relations, peacekeeping, and humanitarian action. He presently serves as executive director of the Academic Council on the United Nations System.

The Sponsoring Institutions

Brown University's **Thomas J. Watson Jr. Institute for International Studies** was established in 1986 to ensure that the university continuously develop its international dimension for the benefit of students and faculty, and, ultimately, society. Based in Providence, R.I., the Watson Institute provides a university-wide focus for teaching and research on international relationships and foreign cultures and societies, and is the focal point for generating support for international studies, setting priorities, and implementing plans. It provides financial support for faculty teaching and research, and sponsors lectures, conferences, and visiting fellows. Its thirteen affiliated centers and programs are engaged in a broad range of activities, from improving the teaching of international studies to contributing to policy-oriented research and public outreach. The Watson Institute provides material support for the university's libraries, promotes faculty development, and advises on international programs.

The **Refugee Policy Group** was established in 1982 as an independent center for policy research and analysis on international and domestic refugee issues. RPG serves as a catalyst for policy improvements by enhancing the quality of information and analysis available to decision-makers concerned with refugee and related humanitarian issues. RPG promotes increased understanding of the broader contexts in which refugee problems occur so that issues can be addressed in a longer-range and more comprehensive manner. It promotes evenhanded, less ideologically based policies that give first priority to humanitarian considerations. RPG serves as a center for the exchange of information and symposia and policy briefings. Its Resource Center, which contains more than 20,000 documents, is open to policy analysts and scholars. RPG is headquartered in Washington, D.C., with an office in Geneva, Switzerland.

Index

103